La Saisiaz & The Two Poets of Croisic by Robert Browning

Robert Browning is one of the most significant Victorian Poets and, of course, English Poetry.

Much of his reputation is based upon his mastery of the dramatic monologue although his talents encompassed verse plays and even a well-regarded essay on Shelley during a long and prolific career.

He was born on May 7th, 1812 in Walmouth, London. Much of his education was home based and Browning was an eclectic and studious student, learning several languages and much else across a myriad of subjects, interests and passions.

Browning's early career began promisingly. The fragment from his intended long poem Pauline brought him to the attention of Dante Gabriel Rossetti, and was followed by Paracelsus, which was praised by both William Wordsworth and Charles Dickens. In 1840 the difficult Sordello, which was seen as willfully obscure, brought his career almost to a standstill.

Despite these artistic and professional difficulties his personal life was about to become immensely fulfilling. He began a relationship with, and then married, the older and better known Elizabeth Barrett. This new foundation served to energise his writings, his life and his career.

During their time in Italy they both wrote much of their best work. With her untimely death in 1861 he returned to London and thereafter began several further major projects.

The collection Dramatis Personae (1864) and the book-length epic poem The Ring and the Book (1868-69) were published and well received; his reputation as a venerated English poet now assured.

Robert Browning died in Venice on December 12th, 1889.

Index of Contents

LA SAISIAZ

DEDICATED TO MRS. SUTHERLAND ORR

Miss A. Egerton-Smith was, at the time of her death, one of Browning's oldest women friends. "He first met her," says Mrs. Sutherland Orr, "as a young woman in Florence when she was visiting there; and the love for and proficiency in music soon asserted itself as a bond of sympathy between them. They did not, however, see much of each other till he had finally left Italy, and she also had made her home in London.... Mr. Browning was one of the very few persons whose society she cared to cultivate: and for many years the common musical interest took the practical, and for both of them convenient, form, of their going to concerts together." Browning was at La Saisiaz, under the Salève, when Miss Egerton-Smith, who was also domiciled there, died suddenly in the autumn of 1877, and it was after the shock of her loss that he composed the poem to which he gave the title of their summer resort. The poem is dated November 9, 1877.

Good, to forgive;
  Best, to forget!
  Living, we fret;
Dying, we live.
Fretless and free,
  Soul, clap thy pinion!
  Earth have dominion,
Body, o'er thee!

Wander at will,
  Day after day,—
  Wander away,
Wandering still—
Soul that canst soar!
  Body may slumber:
  Body shall cumber
Soul-flight no more.

Waft of soul's wing!
  What lies above?
  Sunshine and Love,
Skyblue and Spring!
Body hides—where?
  Ferns of all feather,
  Mosses and heather,
Yours be the care!

LA SAISIAZ

A. E. S. SEPTEMBER 14, 1877.

Dared and done: at last I stand upon the summit, Dear and True!
Singly dared and done; the climbing both of us were bound to do.
Petty feat and yet prodigious: every side my glance was bent
O'er the grandeur and the beauty lavished through the whole ascent.
Ledge by ledge, out broke new marvels, now minute and now immense:
Earth's most exquisite disclosure, heaven's own God in evidence!
And no berry in its hiding, no blue space in its outspread,
Pleaded to escape my footstep, challenged my emerging head,
(As I climbed or paused from climbing, now o'erbranched by shrub and tree,
Now built round by rock and boulder, now at just a turn set free,

Stationed face to face with—Nature? rather with Infinitude,)
—No revealment of them all, as singly I my path pursued,
But a bitter touched its sweetness, for the thought stung "Even so
Both of us had loved and wondered just the same, five days ago!"
Five short days, sufficient hardly to entice, from out its den
Splintered in the slab, this pink perfection of the cyclamen;
Scarce enough to heal and coat with amber gum the sloe-tree's gash,
Bronze the clustered wilding apple, redden ripe the mountain-ash:
Yet of might to place between us—Oh the barrier! Yon Profound
Shrinks beside it, proves a pin-point: barrier this, without a   bound!
Boundless though it be, I reach you: somehow seem to have you here
—Who are there. Yes, there you dwell now, plain the four low walls appear;
Those are vineyards, they enclose from; and the little spire which points
—That's Collonge, henceforth your dwelling. All the same, howe'er disjoints
Past from present, no less certain you are here, not there: have dared,
Done the feat of mountain-climbing;,—five days since, we both prepared
Daring, doing, arm in arm, if other help should haply fail.
For you asked, as forth we sallied to see sunset from the vale,
"Why not try for once the mountain,—take a foretaste, snatch by stealth
Sight and sound, some unconsidered fragment of the hoarded wealth?
Six weeks at its base, yet never once have we together won
Sight or sound by honest climbing: let us two have dared and done
Just so much of twilight journey as may prove to-morrow's jaunt
Not the only mode of wayfare—wheeled to reach the eagle's haunt!"
So, we turned from the low grass-path you were pleased to call "your own,"
Set our faces to the rose-bloom o'er the summit's front of stone
Where Salève obtains, from Jura and the sunken sun she hides,
Due return of blushing "Good Night," rosy as a borne-off bride's,
For his masculine "Good Morrow" when, with sunrise still in hold,
Gay he hails her, and, magnific, thrilled her black length burns to gold.
Up and up we went, how careless—nay, how joyous! All was new,
All was strange. "Call progress toilsome? that were just insulting you!
How the trees must temper noontide! Ah, the thicket's sudden break!
What will be the morning glory, when at dusk thus gleams the lake?
Light by light puts forth Geneva: what a land—and, of the land,
Can there be a lovelier station than this spot where now we stand?
Is it late, and wrong to linger? True, to-morrow makes amends.
Toilsome progress? child's play, call it—specially when one descends!
There, the dread descent is over—hardly our adventure, though!
Take the vale where late we left it, pace the grass-path, 'mine,' you know!
Proud completion of achievement!" And we paced it, praising still
That soft tread on velvet verdure as it wound through hill and hill;
And at very end there met us, coming from Collonge, the pair
—All our people of the Chalet—two, enough and none to spare.
So, we made for home together, and we reached it as the stars
One by one came lamping—chiefly that prepotency of Mars—
And your last word was "I owe you this enjoyment!"—met with "Nay:
With yourself it rests to have a month of morrows like to-day!"

Then the meal, with talk and laughter, and the news of that rare nook
Yet untroubled by the tourist, touched on by no travel-book,
All the same—though latent—patent, hybrid birth of land and sea,
And (our travelled friend assured you)—if such miracle might be—
Comparable for completeness of both blessings—all around
Nature, and, inside her circle, safety from world's sight and sound—
Comparable to our Saisiaz. "Hold it fast and guard it well!
Go and see and vouch for certain, then come back and never tell
Living soul but us; and haply, prove our sky from cloud as clear,
There may we four meet, praise fortune just as now, another year!"

Thus you charged him on departure: not without the final charge,
"Mind to-morrow's early meeting! We must leave our journey marge
Ample for the wayside wonders: there 's the stoppage at the inn
Three-parts up the mountain, where the hardships of the track begin;
There 's the convent worth a visit; but, the triumph crowning all—
There 's Saleve's own platform facing glory which strikes greatness small,
—Blanc, supreme above his earth-brood, needles red and white and green,
Horns of silver, fangs of crystal set on edge in his demesne.
So, some three weeks since, we saw them: so, to-morrow we intend
You shall see them likewise; therefore Good Night till to-morrow, friend!"
Last, the nothings that extinguish embers of a vivid day:
"What might be the Marshal's next move, what Gambetta's counter-play?"
Till the landing on the staircase saw escape the latest spark:
"Sleep you well!" "Sleep but as well, you!"—lazy love quenched, all was dark.

Nothing dark next day at sundawn! Up I rose and forth I fared:
Took my plunge within the bath-pool, pacified the watch-dog scared,
Saw proceed the transmutation—Jura's black to one gold glow,
Trod your level path that let me drink the morning deep and slow,
Reached the little quarry—ravage recompensed by shrub and fern—
Till the overflowing ardors told me time was for return.
So, return I did, and gayly. But, for once, from no far mound
Waved salute a tall white figure. "Has her sleep been so profound?
Foresight, rather, prudent saving strength for day's expenditure!
Ay, the chamber-window 's open: out and on the terrace, sure!"

No, the terrace showed no figure, tall, white, leaning through the wreaths,
Tangle-twine of leaf and bloom that intercept the air one breathes,
Interpose between one's love and Nature's loving, hill and dale
Down to where the blue lake's wrinkle marks the river's inrush pale
—Mazy Arve: whereon no vessel but goes sliding white and plain,
Not a steamboat pants from harbor but one hears pulsate amain,
Past the city's congregated peace of homes and pomp of spires
—Man's mild protest that there 's something more than Nature, man requires,
And that, useful as is Nature to attract the tourist's foot,
Quiet slow sure money-making proves the matter's very root,—
Need for body,—while the spirit also needs a comfort reached

By no help of lake or mountain, but the texts whence Calvin preached.
"Here 's the veil withdrawn from landscape: up to Jura and beyond,
All awaits us ranged and ready; yet she violates the bond,
Neither leans nor looks nor listens: why is this?" A turn of eye
Took the whole sole answer, gave the undisputed reason "why"!

This dread way you had your summons! No premonitory touch,
As you talked and laughed ('t is told me) scarce a minute ere the clutch
Captured you in cold forever. Cold? nay, warm you were as life
When I raised you, while the others used, in passionate poor strife,
All the means that seemed to promise any aid, and all in vain.
Gone you were, and I shall never see that earnest face again
Grow transparent, grow transfigured with the sudden light that leapt
At the first word's provocation, from the heart-deeps where it slept.

Therefore, paying piteous duty, what seemed You have we consigned
Peacefully to—what I think were, of all earth-beds, to your mind
Most the choice for quiet, yonder: low walls stop the vines' approach,
Lovingly Salève protects you; village-sports will ne'er encroach
On the stranger lady's silence, whom friends bore so kind and well
Thither "just for love's sake,"—such their own word was: and who can tell?
You supposed that few or none had known and loved you in the world:
Maybe! flower that 's full-blown tempts the butterfly, not flower that 's furled.
But more learned sense unlocked you, loosed the sheath and let expand
Bud to bell and outspread flower-shape at the least warm touch of hand
—Maybe, throb of heart, beneath which—quickening farther than it knew—
Treasure oft was disembosomed, scent all strange and unguessed hue.
Disembosomed, re-embosomed,—must one memory suffice,
Prove I knew an Alpine-rose which all beside named Edelweiss?

Rare thing, red or white, you rest now: two days slumbered through; and since
One day more will see me rid of this same scene whereat I wince,
Tetchy at all sights and sounds and pettish at each idle charm
Proffered me who pace now singly where we two went arm in arm,—
I have turned upon my weakness: asked, "And what, forsooth, prevents
That, this latest day allowed me, I fulfil of her intents
One she had the most at heart—that we should thus again survey
From Salève Mont Blanc together?" Therefore,—dared and done to-day
Climbing,—here I stand: but you—where?

If a spirit of the place
Broke the silence, bade me question, promised answer,—what disgrace
Did I stipulate "Provided answer suit my hopes, not fears!"
Would I shrink to learn my lifetime's limit—days, weeks, months or years?
Would I shirk assurance on each point whereat I can but guess—
"Does the soul survive the body? Is there God's self, no or yes?"
If I know my mood, 't were constant—come in whatsoe'er uncouth
Shape it should, nay, formidable—so the answer were but truth.

Well, and wherefore shall it daunt me, when 't is I myself am tasked,
When, by weakness weakness questioned, weakly answers—weakly asked?
Weakness never needs be falseness: truth is truth in each degree
—Thunder-pealed by God to Nature, whispered by my soul to me.
Nay, the weakness turns to strength and triumphs in a truth beyond:
"Mine is but man's truest answer—how were it did God respond?"
I shall no more dare to mimic such response in futile speech,
Pass off human lisp as echo of the sphere-song out of reach,
Than,—because it well may happen yonder, where the far snows blanch
Mute Mont Blanc, that who stands near them sees and hears an avalanche,—
I shall pick a clod and throw,—cry, "Such the sight and such the sound!
What though I nor see nor hear them? Others do, the proofs abound!"
Can I make my eye an eagle's, sharpen ear to recognize
Sound o'er league and league of silence? Can I know, who but surmise?
If I dared no self-deception when, a week since, I and you
Walked and talked along the grass-path, passing lightly in review
What seemed hits and what seemed misses in a certain fence-play,—strife
Sundry minds of mark engaged in "On the Soul and Future Life,"—
If I ventured estimating what was come of parried thrust,
Subtle stroke, and, rightly, wrongly, estimating could be just
—Just, though life so seemed abundant in the form which moved by mine,
I might well have played at feigning, fooling,—laughed "What need opine
Pleasure must succeed to pleasure, else past pleasure turns to pain,
And this first life claims a second, else I count its good no gain?"—
Much less have I heart to palter when the matter to decide
Now becomes "Was ending ending once and always, when you died?"
Did the face, the form I lifted as it lay, reveal the loss
Not alone of life but soul? A tribute to yon flowers and moss,
What of you remains beside? A memory! Easy to attest
"Certainly from out the world that one believes who knew her best
Such was good in her, such fair, which fair and good were great perchance
Had but fortune favored, bidden each shy faculty advance;
After all—who knows another? Only as I know, I speak."
So much of you lives within me while I live my year or week.
Then my fellow takes the tale up, not unwilling to aver
Duly in his turn, "I knew him best of all, as he knew her:
Such he was, and such he was not, and such other might have been
But that somehow every actor, somewhere in this earthly scene,
Fails." And so both memories dwindle, yours and mine together linked,
Till there is but left for comfort, when the last spark proves extinct,
This—that somewhere new existence led by men and women new
Possibly attains perfection coveted by me and you;
While ourselves, the only witness to what work our life evolved,
Only to ourselves proposing problems proper to be solved
By ourselves alone,—who working ne'er shall know if work bear fruit
Others reap and garner, heedless how produced by stalk and root,—
We who, darkling, timed the day's birth,—struggling, testified to peace,—

Earned, by dint of failure, triumph,—we, creative thought, must cease
In created word, thought's echo, due to impulse long since sped!
Why repine? There 's ever some one lives although ourselves be dead!

Well, what signifies repugnance? Truth is truth howe'er it strike.
Fair or foul the lot apportioned life on earth, we bear alike.
Stalwart body idly yoked to stunted spirit, powers, that fain
Else would soar, condemned to grovel, groundlings through the fleshly chain,—
Help that hinders, hindrance proved but help disguised when all too late,—
Hindrance is the fact acknowledged, howsoe'er explained as Fate,
Fortune, Providence: we bear, own life a burden more or less.
Life thus owned unhappy, is there supplemental happiness
Possible and probable in life to come? or must we count
Life a curse and not a blessing, summed-up in its whole amount,
Help and hindrance, joy and sorrow?
Why should I want courage here?
I will ask and have an answer,—with no favor, with no fear,—
From myself. How much, how little, do I inwardly believe
True that controverted doctrine? Is it fact to which I cleave,
Is it fancy I but cherish, when I take upon my lips
Phrase the solemn Tuscan fashioned, and declare the soul's eclipse
Not the soul's extinction? take his "I believe and I declare—
Certain am I—from this life I pass into a better, there
Where that lady lives of whom enamored was my soul"—where this
Other lady, my companion dear and true, she also is?

I have questioned and am answered. Question, answer presuppose
Two points: that the thing itself which questions, answers,—is, it knows;
As it also knows the thing perceived outside itself,—a force
Actual ere its own beginning, operative through its course,
Unaffected by its end,—that this thing likewise needs must be;
Call this—God, then, call that—soul, and both—the only facts for me.
Prove them facts? that they o'erpass my power of proving, proves them such:
Fact it is I know I know not something which is fact as much.
What before caused all the causes, what effect of all effects
Haply follows,—these are fancy. Ask the rush if it suspects
Whence and how the stream which floats it had a rise, and where and how
Falls or flows on still! What answer makes the rush except that now
Certainly it floats and is, and, no less certain than itself,
Is the everyway external stream that now through shoal and shelf
Floats it onward, leaves it—maybe—wrecked at last, or lands on shore
There to root again and grow and flourish stable evermore.
—Maybe! mere surmise not knowledge: much conjecture styled belief,
What the rush conceives the stream means through the voyage blind and brief.
Why, because I doubtless am, shall I as doubtless be? "Because
God seems good and wise." Yet under this our life's apparent laws
Reigns a wrong which, righted once, would give quite other laws to life.
"He seems potent." Potent here, then: why are right and wrong at strife?

Has in life the wrong the better? Happily life ends so soon!
Right predominates in life? Then why two lives and double boon?
"Anyhow, we want it: wherefore want?" Because, without the want,
Life, now human, would be brutish: just that hope, however scant,
Makes the actual life worth leading; take the hope therein away,
All we have to do is surely not endure another day.
This life has its hopes for this life, hopes that promise joy: life done—
Out of all the hopes, how many had complete fulfilment? None.
"But the soul is not the body:" and the breath is not the flute;
Both together make the music: either marred and all is mute.
Truce to such old sad contention whence, according as we shape
Most of hope or most of fear, we issue in a half-escape:
"We believe" is sighed. I take the cup of comfort proffered thus,
Taste and try each soft ingredient, sweet infusion, and discuss
What their blending may accomplish for the cure of doubt, till—slow,
Sorrowful, but how decided! needs must I o'erturn it—so!
Cause before, effect behind me—blanks! The midway point I am,
Caused, itself—itself efficient: in that narrow space must cram
All experience—out of which there crowds conjecture manifold,
But, as knowledge, this comes only—things may be as I behold,
Or may not be, but, without me and above me, things there are;
I myself am what I know not—ignorance which proves no bar
To the knowledge that I am, and, since I am, can recognize
What to me is pain and pleasure: this is sure, the rest—surmise.
If my fellows are or are not, what may please them and what pain,—
Mere surmise: my own experience—that is knowledge, once again!

I have lived, then, done and suffered, loved and hated, learnt and taught
This—there is no reconciling wisdom with a world distraught,
Goodness with triumphant evil, power with failure in the aim,
If—(to my own sense, remember! though none other feel the same!)
If you bar me from assuming earth to be a pupil's place,
And life, time—with all their chances, changes—just probation-space,
Mine, for me. But those apparent other mortals—theirs, for them?
Knowledge stands on my experience: all outside its narrow hem,
Free surmise may sport and welcome! Pleasures, pains affect mankind
Just as they affect myself? Why, here 's my neighbor color-blind,
Eyes like mine to all appearance: "green as grass" do I affirm?
"Red as grass" he contradicts me;—which employs the proper term?
Were we two the earth's sole tenants, with no third for referee,
How should I distinguish? Just so, God must judge 'twixt man and me.
To each mortal peradventure earth becomes a new machine,
Pain and pleasure no more tally in our sense than red and green;
Still, without what seems such mortal's pleasure, pain, my life were lost
—Life, my whole sole chance to prove—although at man's apparent cost—
What is beauteous and what ugly, right to strive for, right to shun,
Fit to help and fit to hinder,—prove my forces every one,
Good and evil,—learn life's lesson, hate of evil, love of good,

As 't is set me, understand so much as may be understood—
Solve the problem: "From thine apprehended scheme of things, deduce
Praise or blame of its contriver, shown a niggard or profuse
In each good or evil issue! nor miscalculate alike
Counting one the other in the final balance, which to strike,
Soul was born and life allotted: ay, the show of things unfurled
For thy summing-up and judgment,—thine, no other mortal's world!"

What though fancy scarce may grapple with the complex and immense
—"His own world for every mortal?" Postulate omnipotence!
Limit power, and simple grows the complex: shrunk to atom size,
That which loomed immense to fancy low before my reason lies,—
I survey it and pronounce it work like other work: success
Here and there, the workman's glory,—here and there, his shame no less,
Failure as conspicuous. Taunt not "Human work ape work divine?"
As the power, expect performance! God's be God's as mine is mine!
God whose power made man and made man's wants, and made, to meet those wants,
Heaven and earth which, through the body, prove the spirit's ministrants,
Excellently all,—did he lack power or was the will in fault
When he let blue heaven be shrouded o'er by vapors of the vault,
Gay earth drop her garlands shrivelled at the first infecting breath
Of the serpent pains which herald, swarming in, the dragon death?
What, no way but this that man may learn and lay to heart how rife
Life were with delights would only death allow their taste to life?
Must the rose sigh "Pluck—I perish!" must the eve weep "Gaze—I fade!"
—Every sweet warn "'Ware my bitter!" every shine bid "Wait my shade"?
Can we love but on condition, that the thing we love must die?
Needs there groan a world in anguish just to teach us sympathy—
Multitudinously wretched that we, wretched too, may guess
What a preferable state were universal happiness?
Hardly do I so conceive the outcome of that power which went
To the making of the worm there in yon clod its tenement,
Any more than I distinguish aught of that which, wise and good,
Framed the leaf, its plain of pasture, dropped the dew, its fineless food.
Nay, were fancy fact, were earth and all it holds illusion mere,
Only a machine for teaching love and hate and hope and fear
To myself, the sole existence, single truth 'mid falsehood,—well!
If the harsh throes of the prelude die not off into the swell
Of that perfect piece they sting me to become a-strain for,—if
Roughness of the long rock-clamber lead not to the last of cliff,
First of level country where is sward my pilgrim-foot can prize,—
Plainlier! if this life's conception new life fail to realize,—
Though earth burst and proved a bubble glassing hues of hell, one huge
Reflex of the devil's doings—God's work by no subterfuge—
(So death's kindly touch informed me as it broke the glamour, gave
Soul and body both release from life's long nightmare in the grave)—
Still,—with no more Nature, no more Man as riddle to be read,
Only my own joys and sorrows now to reckon real instead,—

I must say—or choke in silence—"Howsoever came my fate,
Sorrow did and joy did nowise—life well weighed—preponderate."
By necessity ordained thus? I shall bear as best I can;
By a cause all-good, all-wise, all-potent? No, as I am man!
Such were God: and was it goodness that the good within my range
Or had evil in admixture or grew evil's self by change?
Wisdom—that becoming wise meant making slow and sure advance
From a knowledge proved in error to acknowledged ignorance?
Power! 't is just the main assumption reason most revolts at! power
Unavailing for bestowment on its creature of an hour,
Man, of so much proper action rightly aimed and reaching aim,
So much passion,—no defect there, no excess, but still the same,—
As what constitutes existence, pure perfection bright as brief
For yon worm, man's fellow-creature, on yon happier world—its leaf!
No, as I am man, I mourn the poverty I must impute:
Goodness, wisdom, power, all bounded, each a human attribute!

But, O world outspread beneath me! only for myself I speak,
Nowise dare to play the spokesman for my brothers strong and weak,
Full and empty, wise and foolish, good and bad, in every age,
Every clime, I turn my eyes from, as in one or other stage
Of a torture writhe they, Job-like couched on dung and crazed with blains
—Wherefore? whereto? ask the whirlwind what the dread voice thence explains!
I shall "vindicate no way of God's to man," nor stand apart,
"Laugh, be candid," while I watch it traversing the human heart!
Traversed heart must tell its story uncommented on: no less
Mine results in, "Only grant a second life; I acquiesce
In this present life as failure, count misfortune's worst assaults
Triumph, not defeat, assured that loss so much the more exalts
Gain about to be. For at what moment did I so advance
Near to knowledge as when frustrate of escape from ignorance?
Did not beauty prove most precious when its opposite obtained
Rule, and truth seem more than ever potent because falsehood reigned?
While for love—Oh how but, losing love, does whoso loves succeed
By the death-pang to the birth-throe—learning what is love indeed?
Only grant my soul may carry high through death her cup unspilled,
Brimming though it be with knowledge, life's loss drop by drop distilled,
I shall boast it mine—the balsam, bless each kindly wrench that wrung
From life's tree its inmost virtue, tapped the root whence pleasure sprung,
Barked the bole, and broke the bough, and bruised the berry, left all grace
Ashes in death's stern alembic, loosed elixir in its place!"

Witness, Dear and True, how little I was 'ware of—not your worth
—That I knew, my heart assures me—but of what a shade on earth
Would the passage from my presence of the tall white figure throw
O'er the ways we walked together! Somewhat narrow, somewhat slow,
Used to seem the ways, the walking: narrow ways are well to tread
When there 's moss beneath the footstep, honeysuckle overhead:

Walking slow to beating bosom surest solace soonest gives,
Liberates the brain o'erloaded—best of all restoratives.
Nay, do I forget the open vast where soon or late converged
Ways though winding?—world-wide heaven-high sea where music slept or surged
As the angel had ascendant, and Beethoven's Titan mace
Smote the immense to storm, Mozart would by a finger's lifting chase?
Yes, I knew—but not with knowledge such as thrills me while I view
Yonder precinct which henceforward holds and hides the Dear and True.
Grant me (once again) assurance we shall each meet each some day,
Walk—but with how bold a footstep! on a way—but what a way!
—Worst were best, defeat were triumph, utter loss were utmost gain.
Can it be, and must, and will it?

Silence! Out of fact's domain,
Just surmise prepared to mutter hope, and also fear—dispute
Fact's inexorable ruling, "Outside fact, surmise be mute!" Well!
Ay, well and best, if fact's self I may force the answer from!
'T is surmise I stop the mouth of! Not above in yonder dome
All a rapture with its rose-glow,—not around, where pile and peak
Strainingly await the sun's fall,—not beneath, where crickets creak,
Birds assemble for their bedtime, soft the treetop swell subsides,—
No, nor yet within my deepest sentient self the knowledge hides.
Aspiration, reminiscence, plausibilities of trust
—Now the ready "Man were wronged else," now the rash "and God unjust"—
None of these I need. Take thou, my soul, thy solitary stand,
Umpire to the champions Fancy, Reason, as on either hand
Amicable war they wage and play the foe in thy behoof!
Fancy thrust and Reason parry! Thine the prize who stand aloof!

FANCY

I concede the thing refused: henceforth no certainty more plain
Than this mere surmise that after body dies soul lives again.
Two, the only facts acknowledged late, are now increased to three—
God is, and the soul is, and, as certain, after death shall be.
Put this third to use in life, the time for using fact!

REASON

I do:
Find it promises advantage, coupled with the other two.
Life to come will be improvement on the life that 's now; destroy
Body's thwartings, there 's no longer screen betwixt soul and soul's joy.
Why should we expect new hindrance, novel tether? In this first
Life, I see the good of evil, why our world began at worst:
Since time means amelioration, tardily enough displayed,

Yet a mainly onward moving, never wholly retrograde.
We know more though we know little, we grow stronger though still weak,
Partly see though all too purblind, stammer though we cannot speak.
There is no such grudge in God as scared the ancient Greek, no fresh
Substitute of trap for drag-net, once a breakage in the mesh.
Dragons were, and serpents are, and blindworms will be: ne'er emerged
Any new-created python for man's plague since earth was purged.
Failing proof, then, of invented trouble to replace the old,
O'er this life the next presents advantage much and manifold:
Which advantage—in the absence of a fourth and farther fact
Now conceivably surmised, of harm to follow from the act—
I pronounce for man's obtaining at this moment. Why delay?
Is he happy? happiness will change: anticipate the day!
Is he sad? there 's ready refuge: of all sadness death 's prompt cure!
Is he both, in mingled measure? cease a burden to endure!
Pains with sorry compensations, pleasures stinted in the dole,
Power that sinks and pettiness that soars, all halved and nothing whole,
Idle hopes that lure man onward, forced back by as idle fears—
What a load he stumbles under through his glad sad seventy years,
When a touch sets right the turmoil, lifts his spirit where, flesh-freed,
Knowledge shall be rightly named so, all that seems be truth indeed!
Grant his forces no accession, nay, no faculty's increase,
Only let what now exists continue, let him prove in peace
Power whereof the interrupted unperfected play enticed
Man through darkness, which to lighten any spark of hope sufficed,—
What shall then deter his dying out of darkness into light?
Death itself perchance, brief pain that 's pang, condensed and infinite?
But at worst, he needs must brave it one day, while, at best, he laughs—
Drops a drop within his chalice, sleep not death his science quaffs!
Any moment claims more courage, when, by crossing cold and gloom,
Manfully man quits discomfort, makes for the provided room
Where the old friends want their fellow, where the new acquaintance wait,
Probably for talk assembled, possibly to sup in state!
I affirm and reaffirm it therefore: only make as plain
As that man now lives, that, after dying, man will live again,—
Make as plain the absence, also, of a law to contravene
Voluntary passage from this life to that by change of scene,—
And I bid him—at suspicion of first cloud athwart his sky,
Flower's departure, frost's arrival—never hesitate, but die!

FANCY

Then I double my concession: grant, along with new life sure
This same law found lacking now: ordain that, whether rich or poor
Present life is judged in aught man counts advantage—be it hope,
Be it fear that brightens, blackens most or least his horoscope,—
He, by absolute compulsion such as made him live at all,

Go on living to the fated end of life whate'er befall.
What though, as on earth he darkling grovels, man descry the sphere,
Next life's—call it, heaven of freedom, close above and crystal-clear?
He shall find—say, hell to punish who in aught curtails the term,
Fain would act the butterfly before he has played out the worm!
God, soul, earth, heaven, hell,—five facts now: what is to desiderate?

REASON

Nothing! Henceforth man's existence bows to the monition "Wait!
Take the joys and bear the sorrows—neither with extreme concern!
Living here means nescience simply: 't is next life that helps to learn.
Shut those eyes, next life will open,—stop those ears, next life will teach
Hearing's office,—close those lips, next life will give the power of speech!
Or, if action more amuse thee than the passive attitude,
Bravely bustle through thy being, busy thee for ill or good,
Reap this life's success or failure! Soon shall things be unperplexed
And the right and wrong, now tangled, lie unravelled in the next."

FANCY

Not so fast! Still more concession! not alone do I declare
Life must needs be borne,—I also will that man become aware
Life has worth incalculable, every moment that he spends
So much gain or loss for that next life which on this life depends.
Good, done here, be there rewarded,—evil, worked here, there amerced!
Six facts now, and all established, plain to man the last as first.

REASON

There was good and evil, then, defined to man by this decree?
Was—for at its promulgation both alike have ceased to be.
Prior to this last announcement, "Certainly as God exists,
As He made man's soul, as soul is quenchless by the deathly mists,
Yet is, all the same, forbidden premature escape from time
To eternity's provided purer air and brighter clime,—
Just so certainly depends it on the use to which man turns
Earth, the good or evil done there, whether after death he earns
Life eternal,—heaven, the phrase be, or eternal death,—say, hell.
As his deeds, so proves his portion, doing ill or doing well!"
—Prior to this last announcement, earth was man's probation-place:
Liberty of doing evil gave his doing good a grace;
Once lay down the law, with Nature's simple "Such effects succeed
Causes such, and heaven or hell depends upon man's earthly deed
Just as surely as depends the straight or else the crooked line

On his making point meet point or with or else without incline,"—
Thenceforth neither good nor evil does man, doing what he must.
Lay but down that law as stringent "Wouldst thou live again, be just!"
As this other "Wouldst thou live now, regularly draw thy breath!
For, suspend the operation, straight law's breach results in death"—
And (provided always, man, addressed this mode, be sound and sane)
Prompt and absolute obedience, never doubt, will law obtain!
Tell not me "Look round us! nothing each side but acknowledged law,
Now styled God's—now, Nature's edict!" Where's obedience without flaw
Paid to either? What 's the adage rife in man's mouth? Why, "The best
I both see and praise, the worst I follow "—which, despite professed
Seeing, praising, all the same he follows, since he disbelieves
In the heart of him that edict which for truth his head receives.
There 's evading and persuading and much making law amends
Somehow, there 's the nice distinction 'twixt fast foes and faulty friends,
—Any consequence except inevitable death when, "Die,
Whoso breaks our law!" they publish, God and Nature equally.
Law that 's kept or broken—subject to man's will and pleasure! Whence?
How comes law to bear eluding? Not because of impotence:
Certain laws exist already which to hear means to obey;
Therefore not without a purpose these man must, while those man may
Keep and, for the keeping, haply gain approval and reward.
Break through this last superstructure, all is empty air—no sward
Firm like my first fact to stand on, "God there is, and soul there is,"
And soul's earthly life-allotment: wherein, by hypothesis,
Soul is bound to pass probation, prove its powers, and exercise
Sense and thought on fact, and then, from fact educing fit surmise,
Ask itself, and of itself have solely answer, "Does the scope
Earth affords of fact to judge by warrant future fear or hope?"

Thus have we come back full circle: fancy's footsteps one by one
Go their round conducting reason to the point where they begun,
Left where we were left so lately, Dear and True! When, half a week
Since, we walked and talked and thus I told you, how suffused a cheek
You had turned me had I sudden brought the blush into the smile
By some word like "Idly argued! you know better all the while!"
Now, from me—Oh not a blush, but, how much more, a joyous glow,
Laugh triumphant, would it strike did your "Yes, better I do know"
Break, my warrant for assurance! which assurance may not be
If, supplanting hope, assurance needs must change this life to me.
So, I hope—no more than hope, but hope—no less than hope, because
I can fathom, by no plumb-line sunk in life's apparent laws,
How I may in any instance fix where change should meetly fall
Nor involve, by one revisal, abrogation of them all:
—Which again involves as utter change in life thus law-released,
Whence the good of goodness vanished when the ill of evil ceased.
Whereas, life and laws apparent reinstated,—all we know,
All we know not,—o'er our heaven again cloud closes, until, lo,—

Hope the arrowy, just as constant, comes to pierce its gloom, compelled
By a power and by a purpose which, if no one else beheld,
I behold in life, so—hope!

Sad summing-up of all to say!
Athanasius contra mundum, why should he hope more than they?
So are men made notwithstanding, such magnetic virtue darts
From each head their fancy haloes to their unresisting hearts!
Here I stand, methinks a stone's throw from yon village I this morn
Traversed for the sake of looking one last look at its forlorn
Tenement's ignoble fortune: through a crevice, plain its floor
Piled with provender for cattle, while a dungheap blocked the door.
In that squalid Bossex, under that obscene red roof, arose,
Like a fiery flying serpent from its egg, a soul—Rousseau's.
Turn thence! Is it Diodati joins the glimmer of the lake?
There I plucked a leaf, one week since,—ivy, plucked for Byron's sake.
Famed unfortunates! And yet, because of that phosphoric fame
Swathing blackness' self with brightness till putridity looked flame,
All the world was witched: and wherefore? what could lie beneath, allure
Heart of man to let corruption serve man's head as cynosure?
Was the magic in the dictum "All that 's good is gone and past;
Bad and worse still grows the present, and the worst of all comes last:
Which believe—for I believe it"? So preached one his gospel-news;
While melodious moaned the other, "dying day with dolphin-hues!
Storm, for loveliness and darkness like a woman's eye! Ye mounts
Where I climb to 'scape my fellow, and thou sea wherein he counts
Not one inch of vile dominion! What were your especial-worth
Failed ye to enforce the maxim 'Of all objects found on earth
Man is meanest, much too honored when compared with—what by odds
Beats him—any dog: so, let him go a-howling to his gods!'
Which believe—for I believe it!" Such the comfort man received
Sadly since perforce he must: for why? the famous bard believed!

Fame! Then, give me fame, a moment! As I gather at a glance
Human glory after glory vivifying yon expanse,
Let me grasp them altogether, hold on high and brandish well
Beacon-like above the rapt world ready, whether heaven or hell
Send the dazzling summons earthward, to submit itself the same,
Take on trust the hope or else despair flashed full on face by—Fame!
Thanks, thou pine-tree of Makistos, wide thy giant torch I wave!
Know ye whence I plucked the pillar, late with sky for architrave?
This the trunk, the central solid Knowledge, kindled core, began
Tugging earth-deeps, trying heaven-heights, rooted yonder at Lausanne.
This which flits and spits, the aspic,—sparkles in and out the Boughs
Now, and now condensed, the python, coiling round and round allows
Scarce the bole its due effulgence, dulled by flake on flake of Wit—
Laughter so bejewels Learning,—what but Ferney nourished it?
Nay, nor fear—since every resin feeds the flame—that I dispense

With yon Bossex terebinth-tree's all-explosive Eloquence:
No, be sure! nor, any more than thy resplendency, Jean-Jacques,
Dare I want thine, Diodati! What though monkeys and macaques
Gibber "Byron"? Byron's ivy rears a branch beyond the crew,
Green forever, no deciduous trash macaques and monkeys chew!
As Rousseau, then, eloquent, as Byron prime in poet's power,—
Detonations, fulgurations, smiles—the rainbow, tears—the shower,—
Lo, I lift the coruscating marvel—Fame! and, famed, declare
—Learned for the nonce as Gibbon, witty as wit's self Voltaire ...
Oh, the sorriest of conclusions to whatever man of sense
'Mid the millions stands the unit, takes no flare for evidence!
Yet the millions have their portion, live their calm or troublous day,
Find significance in fireworks: so, by help of mine, they may
Confidently lay to heart and lock in head their life long—this:
"He there with the brand flamboyant, broad o'er night's forlorn abyss,
Crowned by prose and verse; and wielding, with Wit's bauble,
Learning's rod" ...
Well? Why, he at least believed in Soul, was very sure of God!

So the poor smile played, that evening: pallid smile long since extinct
Here in London's mid-November! Not so loosely thoughts were linked,
Six weeks since as I, descending in the sunset from Salève,
Found the chain I seemed to forge there, flawless till it reached your grave,—
Not so filmy was the texture, but I bore it in my breast
Safe thus far. And since I found a something in me would not rest
Till I, link by link, unravelled any tangle of the chain,
—Here it lies, for much or little! I have lived all o'er again
That last pregnant hour: I saved it, just as I could save a root
Disinterred for reinterment when the time best helps to shoot.
Life is stocked with germs of torpid life; but may I never wake
Those of mine whose resurrection could not be without earthquake!
Rest all such, unraised forever! Be this, sad yet sweet, the sole
Memory evoked from slumber! Least part this: then what the whole?

THE TWO POETS OF CROISIC

Written immediately after La Saisiaz, being dated January 15, 1878.

Such a starved bank of moss
Till, that May-morn,
Blue ran the flash across:
Violets were born!

Sky—what a scowl of cloud
Till, near and far,

Ray on ray split the shroud:
Splendid, a star!

World—how it walled about
Life with disgrace
Till God's own smile came out:
That was thy face!

I

"Fame!" Yes, I said it and you read it. First,
Praise the good log-fire! Winter howls without.
Crowd closer, let us! Ha, the secret nursed
Inside yon hollow, crusted roundabout
With copper where the clamp was,—how the burst
Vindicates flame the stealthy feeder! Spout
Thy splendidest—a minute and no more?
So soon again all sobered as before?

II

Nay, for I need to see your face! One stroke
Adroitly dealt, and lo, the pomp revealed!
Fire in his pandemonium, heart of oak
Palatial, where he wrought the works concealed
Beneath the solid-seeming roof I broke,
As redly up and out and off they reeled
Like disconcerted imps, those thousand sparks
From fire's slow tunnelling of vaults and arcs!

III

Up, out, and off, see! Were you never used,—
You now, in childish days or rather nights,—
As I was, to watch sparks fly? not amused
By that old nurse-taught game which gave the sprites
Each one his title and career,—confused
Belief 't was all long over with the flights
From earth to heaven of hero, sage, and bard,
And bade them once more strive for Fame's award?

IV

New long bright life! and happy chance befell—

That I know—when some prematurely lost
Child of disaster bore away the bell
From some too-pampered son of fortune, crossed
Never before my chimney broke the spell!
Octogenarian Keats gave up the ghost,
While—never mind Who was it cumbered earth—
Sank stifled, span-long brightness, in the birth.

V

Well, try a variation of the game!
Our log is old ship-timber, broken bulk.
There 's sea-brine spirits up the brimstone flame,
That crimson-curly spiral proves the hulk
Was saturate with—ask the chloride's name
From somebody who knows! I shall not sulk
If yonder greenish tonguelet licked from brass
Its life, I thought was fed on copperas.

VI

Anyhow, there they flutter! What may be
The style and prowess of that purple one?
Who is the hero other eyes shall see
Than yours and mine? That yellow, deep to dun—
Conjecture how the sage glows, whom not we
But those unborn are to get warmth by! Son
O' the coal,—as Job and Hebrew name a spark,—
What bard, in thy red soaring, scares the dark?

VII

Oh and the lesser lights, the dearer still
That they elude a vulgar eye, give ours
The glimpse repaying astronomic skill
Which searched sky deeper, passed those patent powers
Constellate proudly,—swords, scrolls, harps, that fill
The vulgar eye to surfeit,—found best flowers
Hid deepest in the dark,—named unplucked grace
Of soul, ungathered beauty, form or face!

VIII

Up with thee, mouldering ash men never knew,

But I know! flash thou forth, and figure bold,
Calm and columnar as yon flame I view!
Oh and I bid thee,—to whom fortune doled
Scantly all other gifts out—bicker blue,
Beauty for all to see, zinc's uncontrolled
Flake-brilliance! Not my fault if these were shown,
Grandeur and beauty both, to me alone.

IX

No! as the first was boy's play, this proves mere
Stripling's amusement: manhood's sport be grave!
Choose rather sparkles quenched in mid career,
Their boldness and their brightness could not save
(In some old night of time on some lone drear
Sea-coast, monopolized by crag or cave)
—Save from ignoble exit into smoke,
Silence, oblivion, all death-damps that choke!

X

Launched by our ship-wood, float we, once adrift
In fancy to that land-strip waters wash,
We both know well! Where uncouth tribes made shift
Long since to just keep life in, billows dash
Nigh over folk who shudder at each lift
Of the old tyrant tempest's whirlwind-lash
Though they have built the serviceable town
Tempests but tease now, billows drench, not drown.

XI

Croisic, the spit of sandy rock which juts
Spitefully northward, bears nor tree nor shrub
To tempt the ocean, show what Guérande shuts
Behind her, past wild Batz whose Saxons grub
The ground for crystals grown where ocean gluts
Their promontory's breadth with salt: all stub
Of rock and stretch of sand, the land's last strife
To rescue a poor remnant for dear life.

XII

And what life! Here was, from the world to choose,

The Druids' chosen chief of homes: they reared
—Only their women,—'mid the slush and ooze
Of yon low islet,—to their sun, revered
In strange stone guise,—a temple. May-dawn dews
Saw the old structure levelled; when there peered
May's earliest eve-star, high and wide once more
Up towered the new pile perfect as before:

XIII

Seeing that priestesses—and all were such—
Unbuilt and then rebuilt it every May,
Each alike helping—well, if not too much!
For, 'mid their eagerness to outstrip day
And get work done, if any loosed her clutch
And let a single stone drop, straight a prey
Herself fell, torn to pieces, limb from limb,
By sisters in full chorus glad and grim.

XIV

And still so much remains of that gray cult,
That even now, of nights, do women steal
To the sole Menhir standing, and insult
The antagonistic church-spire by appeal
To power discrowned in vain, since each adult
Believes the gruesome thing she clasps may heal
Whatever plague no priestly help can cure:
Kiss but the cold stone, the event is sure!

XV

Nay more: on May-morns, that primeval rite
Of temple-building, with its punishment
For rash precipitation, lingers, spite
Of all remonstrance; vainly are they shent,
Those girls who form a ring and, dressed in white,
Dance round it, till some sister's strength be spent:
Touch but the Menhir, straight the rest turn roughs
From gentles, fall on her with fisticuffs.

XVI

Oh and, for their part, boys from door to door

Sing unintelligible words to tunes
As obsolete: "scraps of Druidic lore,"
Sigh scholars, as each pale man importunes
Vainly the mumbling to speak plain once more.
Enough of this old worship, rounds and runes!
They serve my purpose, which is but to show
Croisic to-day and Croisic long ago.

XVII

What have we sailed to see, then, wafted there
By fancy from the log that ends its days
Of much adventure 'neath skies foul or fair,
On waters rough or smooth, in this good blaze
We two crouch round so closely, bidding care
Keep outside with the snow-storm? Something says
"Fit time for story-telling!" I begin—
Why not at Croisic, port we first put in?

XVIII

Anywhere serves: for point me out the place
Wherever man has made himself a home,
And there I find the story of our race
In little, just at Croisic as at Rome.
What matters the degree? the kind I trace.
Druids their temple, Christians have their dome:
So with mankind; and Croisic, I 'll engage,
With Rome yields sort for sort, in age for age.

XIX

No doubt, men vastly differ: and we need
Some strange exceptional benevolence
Of nature's sunshine to develop seed
So well, in the less-favored clime, that thence
We may discern how shrub means tree indeed
Though dwarfed till scarcely shrub in evidence.
Man in the ice-house or the hot-house ranks
With beasts or gods: stove-forced, give warmth the thanks!

XX

While, is there any ice-checked? Such shall learn

I am thankworthy, who propose to slake
His thirst for tasting how it feels to turn
Cedar from hyssop-on-the-wall. I wake
No memories of what is harsh and stern
In ancient Croisic-nature, much less rake
The ashes of her last warmth till out leaps
Live Hervé Riel, the single spark she keeps.

XXI

Take these two, see, each outbreak,—spirt and spirt
Of fire from our brave billet's either edge
Which—call maternal Croisic ocean-girt!
These two shall thoroughly redeem my pledge.
One flames fierce gules, its feebler rival—vert,
Heralds would tell you: heroes, I allege,
They both were: soldiers, sailors, statesmen, priests,
Lawyers, physicians—guess what gods or beasts!

XXII

None of them all, but—poets, if you please!
"What, even there, endowed with knack of rhyme,
Did two among the aborigines
Of that rough region pass the ungracious time
Suiting, to rumble-tumble of the sea's,
The songs forbidden a serener clime?
Or had they universal audience—that's
To say, the folk of Croisic, ay, and Batz?"

XXIII

Open your ears! Each poet in his day
Had such a mighty moment of success
As pinnacled him straight, in full display,
For the whole world to worship—nothing less!
Was not the whole polite world Paris, pray?
And did not Paris, for one moment—yes,
Worship these poet-flames, our red and green,
One at a time, a century between?

XXIV

And yet you never heard their names! Assist,

Clio, Historic Muse, while I record
Great deeds! Let fact, not fancy, break the mist
And bid each sun emerge, in turn play lord
Of day, one moment! Hear the annalist
Tell a strange story, true to the least word!
At Croisic, sixteen hundred years and ten
Since Christ, forth flamed yon liquid ruby, then.

XXV

Know him henceforth as René Gentilhomme
—Appropriate appellation! noble birth
And knightly blazon, the device wherefrom
Was "Better do than say"! In Croisic's dearth
Why prison his career while Christendom
Lay open to reward acknowledged worth?
He therefore left it at the proper age
And got to be the Prince of Condé's page.

XXVI

Which Prince of Condé, whom men called "The Duke,"
—Failing the king, his cousin, of an heir,
(As one might hold hap, would, without rebuke,
Since Anne of Austria, all the world was ware,
Twenty-three years long sterile, scarce could look
For issue)—failing Louis of so rare
A godsend, it was natural the Prince
Should hear men call him "Next King" too, nor wince.

XXVII

Now, as this reasonable hope, by growth
Of years, nay, tens of years, looked plump almost
To bursting,—would the brothers, childless both,
Louis and Gaston, give but up the ghost—
Condé, called "Duke" and "Next King," nothing loth
Awaited his appointment to the post,
And wiled away the time, as best he might,
Till Providence should settle things aright.

XXVIII

So, at a certain pleasure-house, withdrawn

From cities where a whisper breeds offence,
He sat him down to watch the streak of dawn
Testify to first stir of Providence;
And, since dull country life makes courtiers yawn,
There wanted not a poet to dispense
Song's remedy for spleen-fits all and some,
Which poet was Page René Gentilhomme.

XXIX

A poet born and bred, his very sire
A poet also, author of a piece
Printed and published, "Ladies—their attire:"
Therefore the son, just born at his decease,
Was bound to keep alive the sacred fire,
And kept it, yielding moderate increase
Of songs and sonnets, madrigals, and much
Rhyming thought poetry and praised as such.

XXX

Rubbish unutterable (bear in mind!)
Rubbish not wholly without value, though,
Being to compliment the Duke designed
And bring the complimenter credit so,—
Pleasure with profit happily combined.
Thus René Gentilhomme rhymed, rhymed till—lo,
This happened, as he sat in an alcove
Elaborating rhyme for "love"—not "dove."

XXXI

He was alone: silence and solitude
Befit the votary of the Muse. Around,
Nature—not our new picturesque and rude,
But trim tree-cinctured stately garden-ground—
Breathed polish and politeness. All-imbued
With these, he sat absorbed in one profound
Excogitation, "Were it best to hint
Or boldly boast 'She loves me—Araminte'?"

XXXII

When suddenly flashed lightning, searing sight

Almost, so close to eyes; then, quick on flash,
Followed the thunder, splitting earth downright
Where René sat a-rhyming: with huge crash
Of marble into atoms infinite—
Marble which, stately, dared the world to dash
The stone-thing proud, high-pillared, from its place:
One flash, and dust was all that lay at base.

XXXIII

So, when the horrible confusion loosed
Its wrappage round his senses, and, with breath,
Seeing and hearing by degrees induced
Conviction what he felt was life, not death—
His fluttered faculties came back to roost
One after one, as fowls do: ay, beneath,
About his very feet there, lay in dust
Earthly presumption paid by heaven's disgust.

XXXIV

For, what might be the thunder-smitten thing
But, pillared high and proud, in marble guise,
A ducal crown—which meant "Now Duke: Next, King"?
Since such the Prince was, not in his own eyes
Alone, but all the world's. Pebble from sling
Prostrates a giant; so can pulverize
Marble pretension—how much more, make moult
A peacock-prince his plume—God's thunderbolt!

XXXV

That was enough, for René, that first fact
Thus flashed into him. Up he looked: all blue
And bright the sky above; earth firm, compact
Beneath his footing, lay apparent too;
Opposite stood the pillar: nothing lacked
There, but the Duke's crown: see, its fragments strew
The earth,—about his feet lie atoms fine
Where he sat nursing late his fourteenth line!

XXXVI

So, for the moment, all the universe

Being abolished, all 'twist God and him,—
Earth's praise or blame, its blessing or its curse.
Of one and the same value,—to the brim
Flooded with truth, for better or for worse,—
He pounces on the writing-paper, prim
Keeping its place on table: not a dint
Nor speck had damaged "Ode to Araminte."

XXXVII

And over the neat crowquill calligraph
His pen goes blotting, blurring, as an ox
Tramples a flower-bed in a garden,—laugh
You may!—so does not he, whose quick heart knocks
Audibly at his breast: an epitaph
On earth's break-up, amid the falling rocks,
He might be penning in a wild dismay,
Caught with his work half-done on Judgment Day.

XXXVIII

And what is it so terribly he pens,
Ruining "Cupid, Venus, wile and smile,
Hearts, darts," and all his day's divinior mens
Judged necessary to a perfect style?
Little recks René, with a breast to cleanse,
Of Rhadamanthine law that reigned erewhile:
Brimful of truth, truth's outburst will convince
(Style or no style) who bears truth's brunt—the Prince.

XXXIX

"Condé, called 'Duke,' be called just 'Duke,' not more,
To life's end! 'Next King' thou forsooth wilt be?
Ay, when this bauble, as it decked before
Thy pillar, shall again, for France to see,
Take its proud station there! Let France adore
No longer an illusive mock-sun—thee—
But keep her homage for Sol's self, about
To rise and put pretenders to the rout!

XL

"What? France so God-abandoned that her root

Regal, though many a Spring it gave no sign,
Lacks power to make the bole, now branchless, shoot
Greenly as ever? Nature, though benign,
Thwarts ever the ambitious and astute.
In store for such is punishment condign:
Sure as thy Duke's crown to the earth was hurled,
So sure, next year, a Dauphin glads the world!"

XLI

Which penned—some forty lines to this effect—
Our René folds his paper, marches brave
Back to the mansion, luminous, erect,
Triumphant, an emancipated slave.
There stands the Prince. "How now? My Duke's-crown wrecked?
What may this mean?" The answer René gave
Was—handing him the verses, with the due
Incline of body: "Sir, God's word to you!"

XLII

The Prince read, paled, was silent; all around,
The courtier-company, to whom he passed
The paper, read, in equal silence bound.
René grew also by degrees aghast
At his own fit of courage—palely found
Way of retreat from that pale presence: classed
Once more among the cony-kind. "Oh, son,
It is a feeble folk!" saith Solomon.

XLIII

Vainly he apprehended evil: since,
When, at the year's end, even as foretold,
Forth came the Dauphin who discrowned the Prince
Of that long-craved mere visionary gold,
'T was no fit time for envy to evince
Malice, be sure! The timidest grew bold:
Of all that courtier-company not one
But left the semblance for the actual sun.

XLIV

And all sorts and conditions that stood by

At René's burning moment, bright escape
Of soul, bore witness to the prophecy.
Which witness took the customary shape
Of verse; a score of poets in full cry
Hailed the inspired one. Nantes and Tours agape,
Soon Paris caught the infection; gaining strength,
How could it fail to reach the Court at length?

XLV

"O poet!" smiled King Louis, "and besides,
O prophet! Sure, by miracle announced,
My babe will prove a prodigy. Who chides
Henceforth the unchilded monarch shall be trounced
For irreligion: since the fool derides
Plain miracle by which this prophet pounced
Exactly on the moment I should lift
Like Simeon, in my arms, a babe, 'God's gift!'

XLVI

"So call the boy! and call this bard and seer
By a new title! him I raise to rank
Of 'Royal Poet:' poet without peer!
Whose fellows only have themselves to thank
If humbly they must follow in the rear
My René. He 's the master: they must clank
Their chains of song, confessed his slaves; for why?
They poetize, while he can prophesy!"

XLVII

So said, so done; our René rose august,
"The Royal Poet;" straightway put in type
His poem-prophecy, and (fair and just
Procedure) added,—now that time was ripe
For proving friends did well his word to trust,—
Those attestations, tuned to lyre or pipe,
Which friends broke out with when he dared foretell
The Dauphin's birth: friends trusted, and did well.

XLVIII

Moreover he got painted by Du Pré,

Engraved by Daret also; and prefixed
The portrait to his book: a crown of bay
Circled his brows, with rose and myrtle mixed;
And Latin verses, lovely in their way,
Described him as "the biforked hill betwixt:
Since he hath scaled Parnassus at one jump,
Joining the Delphic quill and Getic trump."

XLIX

Whereof came ... What, it lasts, our spirt, thus long
—The red fire? That 's the reason must excuse
My letting flicker René's prophet-song
No longer; for its pertinacious hues
Must fade before its fellow joins the throng
Of sparks departed up the chimney, dues
To dark oblivion. At the word, it winks,
Rallies, relapses, dwindles, deathward sinks.

L

So does our poet. All this burst of fame,
Fury of favor, Royal Poetship,
Prophetship, book, verse, picture—thereof came
—Nothing! That 's why I would not let outstrip
Red his green rival flamelet: just the same
Ending in smoke waits both! In vain we rip
The past, no further faintest trace remains
Of René to reward our pious pains.

LI

Somebody saw a portrait framed and glazed
At Croisic. "Who may be this glorified
Mortal unheard-of hitherto?" amazed
That person asked the owner by his side,
Who proved as ignorant. The question raised
Provoked inquiry; key by key was tried
On Croisic's portrait-puzzle, till back flew
The wards at one key's touch, which key was—Who?

LII

The other famous poet! Wait thy turn,

Thou green, our red's competitor! Enough
Just now to note 't was he that itched to learn
(A hundred years ago) how fate could puff
Heaven-high (a hundred years before), then spurn
To suds so big a bubble in some huff:
Since green too found red's portrait,—having heard
Hitherto of red's rare self not one word.

LIII

And he with zeal addressed him to the task
Of hunting out, by all and any means,
—Who might the brilliant bard be, born to bask
Butterfly-like in shine which kings and queens
And baby-dauphins shed? Much need to ask!
Is fame so fickle that what perks and preens
The eyed wing, one imperial minute, dips
Next sudden moment into blind eclipse?

LIV

After a vast expenditure of pains,
Our second poet found the prize he sought:
Urged in his search by something that restrains
From undue triumph famed ones who have fought,
Or simply, poetizing, taxed their brains:
Something that tells such—dear is triumph bought
If it means only basking in the midst
Of fame's brief sunshine, as thou, René, didst.

LV

For, what did searching find at last but this?
Quoth somebody, "I somehow somewhere seem
To think I heard one old De Chevaye is
Or was possessed of René's works!" which gleam
Of light from out the dark proved not amiss
To track, by correspondence on the theme;
And soon the twilight broadened into day,
For thus to question answered De Chevaye.

LVI

"True it is, I did once possess the works

You want account of—works—to call them so,—
Comprised in one small book: the volume lurks
(Some fifty leaves in duodecimo)
'Neath certain ashes which my soul it irks
Still to remember, because long ago
That and my other rare shelf-occupants
Perished by burning of my house at Nantes.

LVII

"Yet of that book one strange particular
Still stays in mind with me"—and thereupon
Followed the story. "Few the poems are;
The book was two-thirds filled up with this one,
And sundry witnesses from near and far
That here at least was prophesying done
By prophet, so as to preclude all doubt,
Before the thing he prophesied about."

LVIII

That 's all he knew, and all the poet learned,
And all that you and I are like to hear
Of René; since not only book is burned
But memory extinguished,—nay, I fear,
Portrait is gone too: nowhere I discerned
A trace of it at Croisic. "Must a tear
Needs fall for that?" you smile. "How fortune fares
With such a mediocrity, who cares?"

LIX

Well, I care—intimately care to have
Experience how a human creature felt
In after-life, who bore the burden grave
Of certainly believing God had dealt
For once directly with him: did not rave
—A maniac, did not find his reason melt
—An idiot, but went on, in peace or strife,
The world's way, lived an ordinary life.

LX

How many problems that one fact would solve!

An ordinary soul, no more, no less,
About whose life earth's common sights revolve,
On whom is brought to bear, by thunder-stress,
This fact—God tasks him, and will not absolve
Task's negligent performer! Can you guess
How such a soul—the task performed to point—
Goes back to life nor finds things out of joint?

LXI

Does he stand stock-like henceforth? or proceed
Dizzily, yet with course straightforward still,
Down-trampling vulgar hindrance?—as the reed
Is crushed beneath its tramp when that blind will
Hatched in some old-world beast's brain bids it speed
Where the sun wants brute-presence to fulfil
Life's purpose in a new far zone, ere ice
Enwomb the pasture-tract its fortalice.

LXII

I think no such direct plain truth consists
With actual sense and thought and what they take
To be the solid walls of life: mere mists—
How such would, at that truth's first piercing, break
Into the nullity they are!—slight lists
Wherein the puppet-champions wage, for sake
Of some mock-mistress, mimic war: laid low
At trumpet-blast, there 's shown the world, one foe!

LXIII

No, we must play the pageant out, observe
The tourney-regulations, and regard
Success—to meet the blunted spear nor swerve,
Failure—to break no bones yet fall on sward;
Must prove we have—not courage? well then—nerve!
And, at the day's end, boast the crown's award—
Be warranted as promising to wield
Weapons, no sham, in a true battlefield.

LXIV

Meantime, our simulated thunderclaps

Which tell us counterfeited truths—these same
Are—sound, when music storms the soul, perhaps?
—Sight, beauty, every dart of every aim
That touches just, then seems, by strange relapse,
To fall effectless from the soul it came
As if to fix its own, but simply smote
And startled to vague beauty more remote?

LXV

So do we gain enough—yet not too much—
Acquaintance with that outer element
Wherein there 's operation (call it such!)
Quite of another kind than we the pent
On earth are proper to receive. Our hutch
Lights up at the least chink: let roof be rent—
How inmates huddle, blinded at first spasm,
Cognizant of the sun's self through the chasm!

LXVI

Therefore, who knows if this our René's quick
Subsidence from as sudden noise and glare
Into oblivion was impolitic?
No doubt his soul became at once aware
That, after prophecy, the rhyming-trick
Is poor employment: human praises scare
Rather than soothe ears all a-tingle yet
With tones few hear and live, but none forget.

LXVII

There 's our first famous poet! Step thou forth
Second consummate songster! See, the tongue
Of fire that typifies thee, owns thy worth
In yellow, purple mixed its green among,
No pure and simple resin from the North,
But composite with virtues that belong
To Southern culture! Love not more than hate
Helped to a blaze ... But I anticipate.

LXVIII

Prepare to witness a combustion rich

And riotously splendid, far beyond
Poor René's lambent little streamer which
Only played candle to a Court grown fond
By baby-birth: this soared to such a pitch,
Alternately such colors doffed and donned,
That when I say it dazzled Paris—please
Know that it brought Voltaire upon his knees!

LXIX

Who did it, was a dapper gentleman,
Paul Desforges Maillard, Croisickese by birth,
Whose birth that century ended which began
By similar bestowment on our earth
Of the aforesaid René. Cease to scan
The ways of Providence! See Croisic's dearth—
Not Paris in its plenitude—suffice
To furnish France with her best poet twice!

LXX

Till he was thirty years of age, the vein
Poetic yielded rhyme by drops and spirts:
In verses of society had lain
His talent chiefly; but the Muse asserts
Privilege most by treating with disdain
Epics the bard mouths out, or odes he blurts
Spasmodically forth. Have people time
And patience nowadays for thought in rhyme?

LXXI

So, his achievements were the quatrain's inch
Of homage, or at most the sonnet's ell
Of admiration: welded lines with clinch
Of ending word and word, to every belle
In Croisic's bounds; these, brisk as any finch,
He twittered till his fame had reached as well
Guérande as Batz; but there fame stopped, for—curse
On fortune—outside lay the universe!

LXXII

That 's Paris. Well,—why not break bounds, and send

Song onward till it echo at the gates
Of Paris whither all ambitions tend,
And end too, seeing that success there sates
The soul which hungers most for fame? Why spend
A minute in deciding, while, by Fate's
Decree, there happens to be just the prize
Proposed there, suiting souls that poetize?

LXXIII

A prize indeed, the Academy's own self
Proposes to what bard shall best indite
A piece describing how, through shoal and shelf,
The Art of Navigation; steered aright,
Has, in our last king's reign,—the lucky elf,—
Reached, one may say, Perfection's haven quite,
And there cast anchor. At a glance one sees
The subject's crowd of capabilities!

LXXIV

Neptune and Amphitrité! Thetis, who
Is either Tethys or as good—both tag!
Triton can shove along a vessel too:
It 's Virgil! Then the winds that blow or lag,—
De Maille, Vendôme, Vermandois! Toulouse blew
Longest, we reckon: he must puff the flag
To fullest outflare; while our lacking nymph
Be Anne of Austria, Regent o'er the lymph!

LXXV

Promised, performed! Since irritabilis gens
Holds of the feverish impotence that strives
To stay an itch by prompt resource to pen's
Scratching itself on paper; placid lives,
Leisurely works mark the divinior mens:
Bees brood above the honey in their hives;
Gnats are the busy bustlers. Splash and scrawl,—
Completed lay thy piece, swift penman Paul!

LXXVI

To Paris with the product! This dispatched,

One had to wait the Forty's slow and sure
Verdict, as best one might. Our penman scratched
Away perforce the itch that knows no cure
But daily paper-friction: more than matched
His first feat by a second—tribute pure
And heartfelt to the Forty when their voice
Should peal with one accord "Be Paul our choice!"

LXXVII

Scratch, scratch went much laudation of that sane
And sound Tribunal, delegates august
Of Phœbus and the Muses' sacred train—
Whom every poetaster tries to thrust
From where, high-throned, they dominate the Seine:
Fruitless endeavor,—fail it shall and must!
Whereof in witness have not one and all
The Forty voices pealed "Our choice be Paul"?

LXXVIII

Thus Paul discounted his applause. Alack
For human expectation! Scarcely ink
Was dry when, lo, the perfect piece came back
Rejected, shamed! Some other poet's clink
"Thetis and Tethys" had seduced the pack
Of pedants to declare perfection's pink
A singularly poor production. "Whew!
The Forty are stark fools, I always knew!"

LXXIX

First fury over (for Paul's race—to wit,
Brain-vibrios—wriggle clear of protoplasm
Into minute life that 's one fury-fit),
"These fools shall find a bard's enthusiasm
Comports with what should counterbalance it—
Some knowledge of the world! No doubt, orgasm
Effects the birth of verse which, born, demands
Prosaic ministration, swaddling-bands!

LXXX

"Verse must be cared for at this early stage,

Handled, nay dandled even. I should play
Their game indeed if, till it grew of age,
I meekly let these dotards frown away
My bantling from the rightful heritage
Of smiles and kisses! Let the public say
If it be worthy praises or rebukes,
My poem, from these Forty old perukes!"

LXXXI

So, by a friend, who boasts himself in grace
With no less than the Chevalier La Roque,—
Eminent in those days for pride of place,
Seeing he had it in his power to block
The way or smooth the road to all the race
Of literators trudging up to knock
At Fame's exalted temple-door—for why?
He edited the Paris "Mercury:"—

LXXXII

By this friend's help the Chevalier receives
Paul's poem, prefaced by the due appeal
To Cæsar from the Jews. As duly heaves
A sigh the Chevalier, about to deal
With case so customary—turns the leaves,
Finds nothing there to borrow, beg, or steal—
Then brightens up the critic's brow deep-lined.
"The thing may be so cleverly declined!"

LXXXIII

Down to desk, out with paper, up with quill,
Dip and indite! "Sir, gratitude immense
For this true draught from the Pierian rill!
Our Academic clodpoles must be dense
Indeed to stand unirrigated still.
No less, we critics dare not give offence
To grandees like the Forty: while we mock,
We grin and bear. So, here 's your piece! La Roque."

LXXXIV

"There now!" cries Paul: "the fellow can't avoid

Confessing that my piece deserves the palm;
And yet he dares not grant me space enjoyed
By every scribbler he permits embalm
His crambo in the Journal's corner! Cloyed
With stuff like theirs, no wonder if a qualm
Be caused by verse like mine: though that 's no cause
For his defrauding me of just applause.

LXXXV

"Aha, he fears the Forty, this poltroon?
First let him fear me! Change smooth speech to rough!
I 'll speak my mind out, show the fellow soon
Who is the foe to dread: insist enough
On my own merits till, as clear as noon,
He sees I am no man to take rebuff
As patiently as scribblers may and must!
Quick to the onslaught, out sword, cut and thrust!"

LXXXVI

And thereupon a fierce epistle flings
Its challenge in the critic's face. Alack!
Our bard mistakes his man! The gauntlet rings
On brazen visor proof against attack.
Prompt from his editorial throne up springs
The insulted magnate, and his mace falls, thwack,
On Paul's devoted brainpan,—quite away
From common courtesies of fencing-play!

LXXXVII

"Sir, will you have the truth? This piece of yours
Is simply execrable past belief.
I shrank from saying so; but, since naught cures
Conceit but truth, truth 's at your service! Brief,
Just so long as 'The Mercury' endures,
So long are you excluded by its Chief
From corner, nay, from cranny! Play the cock
O' the roost, henceforth, at Croisic!" wrote La Roque.

LXXXVIII

Paul yellowed, whitened, as his wrath from red

Waxed incandescent. Now, this man of rhyme
Was merely foolish, faulty in the head
Not heart of him: conceit 's a venial crime.
"Oh by no means malicious!" cousins said:
Fussily feeble,—harmless all the time,
Piddling at so-called satire—well-advised,
He held in most awe whom he satirized.

LXXXIX

Accordingly his kith and kin—removed
From emulation of the poet's gift
By power and will—these rather liked, nay, loved
The man who gave his family a lift
Out of the Croisic level; disapproved
Satire so trenchant." Thus our poet sniffed
Home-incense, though too churlish to unlock
"The Mercury's" box of ointment was La Roque.

XC

But when Paul's visage grew from red to white,
And from his lips a sort of mumbling fell
Of who was to be kicked,—"And serve him right!"
A gay voice interposed, "Did kicking well
Answer the purpose! Only—if I might
Suggest as much—a far more potent spell
Lies in another kind of treatment. Oh,
Women are ready at resource, you know!

XCI

"Talent should minister to genius! good:
The proper and superior smile returns.
Hear me with patience! Have you understood
The only method whereby genius earns
Fit guerdon nowadays? In knightly mood
You entered lists with visor up; one learns
Too late that, had you mounted Roland's crest,
'Room!' they had roared—La Roque with all the rest!

XCII

"Why did you first of all transmit your piece

To those same priggish Forty unprepared
Whether to rank you with the swans or geese
By friendly intervention? If they dared
Count you a cackler,—wonders never cease!
I think it still more wondrous that you bared
Your brow (my earlier image) as if praise
Were gained by simple fighting nowadays!

XCIII

"Your next step showed a touch of the true means
Whereby desert is crowned: not force but wile
Came to the rescue. 'Get behind the scenes!'
Your friend advised: he writes, sets forth your style
And title, to such purpose intervenes
That you get velvet-compliment three-pile;
And, though 'The Mercury' said 'nay,' nor stock
Nor stone did his refusal prove La Roque.

XCIV

"Why must you needs revert to the high hand,
Imperative procedure—what you call
'Taking on merit your exclusive stand'?
Stand, with a vengeance! Soon you went to wall.
You and your merit! Only fools command
When folks are free to disobey them, Paul!
You 've learnt your lesson, found out what 's o'clock,
By this uncivil answer of La Roque.

XCV

"Now let me counsel! Lay this piece on shelf
—Masterpiece though it be! From out your desk
Hand me some lighter sample, verse the elf
Cupid inspired you with, no god grotesque
Presiding o'er the Navy! I myself
Hand-write what 's legible yet picturesque;
I 'll copy fair and femininely frock
Your poem masculine that courts La Roque!

XCVI

"Deidamia he—Achilles thou!

Ha, ha, these ancient stories come so apt!
My sex, my youth, my rank I next avow
In a neat prayer for kind perusal. Sapped
I see the walls which stand so stoutly now!
I see the toils about the game entrapped
By honest cunning! Chains of lady's-smock,
Not thorn and thistle, tether fast La Roque!"

XCVII

Now, who might be the speaker sweet and arch
That laughed above Paul's shoulder as it heaved
With the indignant heart?—bade steal a march
And not continue charging? Who conceived
This plan which set our Paul, like pea you parch
On fire-shovel, skipping, of a load relieved,
From arm-chair moodiness to escritoire
Sacred to Phœbus and the tuneful choir?

XCVIII

Who but Paul's sister! named of course like him
"Desforges;" but, mark you, in those days a queer
Custom obtained,—who knows whence grew the whim?—
That people could not read their title clear
To reverence till their own true names, made dim
By daily mouthing, pleased to disappear,
Replaced by brand-new bright ones: Arouet,
For instance, grew Voltaire; Desforges—Malcrais.

XCIX

"Demoiselle Malcrais de la Vigne"—because
The family possessed at Brederac
A vineyard,—few grapes, many hips-and-haws,—
Still a nice Breton name. As breast and back
Of this vivacious beauty gleamed through gauze,
So did her sprightly nature nowise lack
Lustre when draped, the fashionable way,
In "Malcrais de la Vigne,"—more short, "Malcrais."

C

Out from Paul's escritoire behold escape

The hoarded treasure! verse falls thick and fast,
Sonnets and songs of every size and shape.
The lady ponders on her prize; at last
Selects one which—O angel and yet ape!—
Her malice thinks is probably surpassed
In badness by no fellow of the flock,
Copies it fair, and "Now for my La Roque!"

CI

So, to him goes, with the neat manuscript,
The soft petitionary letter. "Grant
A fledgeling novice that with wing unclipt
She soar her little circuit, habitant
Of an old manor; buried in which crypt,
How can the youthful châtelaine but pant
For disemprisonment by one ad hoc
Appointed 'Mercury's' Editor, La Roque?"

CII

'T was an epistle that might move the Turk!
More certainly it moved our middle-aged
Pen-driver drudging at his weary work,
Raked the old ashes up and disengaged
The sparks of gallantry which always lurk
Somehow in literary breasts, assuaged
In no degree by compliments on style;
Are Forty wagging beards worth one girl's smile?

CIII

In trips the lady's poem, takes its place
Of honor in the gratified Gazette,
With due acknowledgment of power and grace;
Prognostication, too, that higher yet
The Breton Muse will soar: fresh youth, high race.
Beauty and wealth have amicably met
That Demoiselle Malcrais may fill the chair
Left vacant by the loss of Deshoulières.

CIV

"There!" cried the lively lady. "Who was right—

You in the dumps, or I the merry maid
Who know a trick or two can baffle spite
Tenfold the force of this old fool's? Afraid
Of Editor La Roque? But come! next flight
Shall outsoar—Deshoulières alone? My blade,
Sappho herself shall you confess outstript!
Quick, Paul, another dose of manuscript!"

CV

And so, once well a-foot, advanced the game:
More and more verses, corresponding gush
On gush of praise, till everywhere acclaim
Rose to the pitch of uproar. "Sappho? Tush!
Sure 'Malcrais on her Parrot' puts to shame
Deshoulières' pastorals, clay not worth a rush
Beside this find of treasure, gold in crock,
Unearthed in Brittany,—nay, ask La Roque!"

CVI

Such was the Paris tribute. "Yes," you sneer,
"Ninnies stock Noodledom, but folk more sage
Resist contagious folly, never fear!"
Do they? Permit me to detach one page
From the huge Album which from far and near
Poetic praises blackened in a rage
Of rapture! and that page shall be—who stares
Confounded now, I ask you?—just Voltaire's!

CVII

Ay, sharpest shrewdest steel that ever stabbed
To death Imposture through the armor-joints!
How did it happen that gross Humbug grabbed
Thy weapons, gouged thine eyes out? Fate appoints
That pride shall have a fall, or I had blabbed
Hardly that Humbug, whom thy soul aroints,
Could thus cross-buttock thee caught unawares,
And dismalest of tumbles proved—Voltaire's!

CVIII

See his epistle extant yet, wherewith

"Henri" in verse and "Charles" in prose he sent
To do her suit and service! Here 's the pith
Of half a dozen stanzas—stones which went
To build that simulated monolith—
Sham love in due degree with homage blent
As sham—which in the vast of volumes scares
The traveller still: "That stucco-heap—Voltaire's?"

CIX

"O thou, whose clarion-voice has overflown
The wilds to startle Paris that 's one ear!
Thou who such strange capacity hast shown
For joining all that 's grand with all that 's dear,
Knowledge with power to please—Deshoulières grown
Learned as Dacier in thy person! mere
Weak fruit of idle hours, these crabs of mine
I dare lay at thy feet, O Muse divine!

CX

"Charles was my task-work only; Henri trod
My hero erst, and now, my heroine—she
Shall be thyself! True—is it true, great God!
Certainly love henceforward must not be!
Yet all the crowd of Fine Arts fail—how odd!—
Tried turn by turn, to fill a void in me!
There 's no replacing love with these, alas!
Yet all I can I do to prove no ass.

CXI

"I labor to amuse my freedom; but
Should any sweet young creature slavery preach,
And—borrowing thy vivacious charm, the slut!—
Make me, in thy engaging words, a speech,
Soon should I see myself in prison shut
With all imaginable pleasure." Reach
The washhand-basin for admirers! There 's
A stomach-moving tribute—and Voltaire's!

CXII

Suppose it a fantastic billet-doux,

Adulatory flourish, not worth frown!
What say you to the Fathers of Trévoux?
These in their Dictionary have her down
Under the heading "Author:" "Malcrais, too,
Is 'Author' of much verse that claims renown."
While Jean-Baptiste Rousseau ... but why proceed?
Enough of this—something too much, indeed!

CXIII

At last La Roque, unwilling to be left
Behindhand in the rivalry, broke bounds
Of figurative passion hilt and heft,
Plunged his huge downright love through what surrounds
The literary female bosom; reft
Away its veil of coy reserve with "Zounds!
I love thee, Breton Beauty! All 's no use!
Body and soul I love,—the big word 's loose!"

CXIV

He 's greatest now and to de-struc-ti-on
Nearest. Attend the solemn word I quote,
O Paul! There 's no pause at per-fec-ti-on.
Thus knolls thy knell the Doctor's bronzèd throat!
Greatness a period hath, no sta-ti-on!
Better and truer verse none ever wrote
(Despite the antique outstretched a-i-on)
Than thou, revered and magisterial Donne!

CXV

Flat on his face, La Roque, and—pressed to heart
His dexter hand—Voltaire with bended knee!
Paul sat and sucked-in triumph; just apart
Leaned over him his sister. "Well?" smirks he,
And "Well?" she answers, smiling—woman's art
To let a man's own mouth, not hers, decree
What shall be next move which decides the game:
Success? She said so. Failure? His the blame.

CXVI

"Well!" this time forth affirmatively comes

With smack of lip, and long-drawn sigh through teeth
Close clenched o'er satisfaction, as the gums
Were tickled by a sweetmeat teased beneath
Palate by lubricating tongue: "Well! crumbs
Of comfort these, undoubtedly! no death
Likely from famine at Fame's feast! 't is clear
I may put claim in for my pittance, Dear!

CXVII

"La Roque, Voltaire, my lovers? Then disguise
Has served its turn, grows idle; let it drop!
I shall to Paris, flaunt there in men's eyes
My proper manly garb and mount a-top
The pedestal that waits me, take the prize
Awarded Hercules. He threw a sop
To Cerberus who let him pass, you know,
Then, following, licked his heels: exactly so!

CXVIII

"I like the prospect—their astonishment,
Confusion: wounded vanity, no doubt,
Mixed motives; how I see the brows quick bent!
'What, sir, yourself, none other, brought about
This change of estimation? Phœbus sent
His shafts as from Diana?' Critic pout
Turns courtier smile: 'Lo, him we took for her!
Pleasant mistake! You bear no malice, sir?'

CXIX

"Eh, my Diana?" But Diana kept
Smilingly silent with fixed needle-sharp
Much-meaning eyes that seemed to intercept
Paul's very thoughts ere they had time to warp
From earnest into sport the words they leapt
To life with—changed as when maltreated harp
Renders in tinkle what some player-prig
Means for a grave tune though it proves a jig.

CXX

"What, Paul, and are my pains thus thrown away,

My lessons end in loss?" at length fall slow
The pitying syllables, her lips allay
The satire of by keeping in full flow,
Above their coral reef, bright smiles at play:
"Can it be, Paul thus fails to rightly know
And altogether estimate applause
As just so many asinine hee-haws?

CXXI

"I thought to show you" ... "Show me," Paul inbroke,
"My poetry is rubbish, and the world
That rings with my renown a sorry joke!
What fairer test of worth than that, form furled,
I entered the arena? Yet you croak
Just as if Phœbé and not Phœbus hurled
The dart and struck the Python! What, he crawls
Humbly in dust before your feet, not Paul's?

CXXII

"Nay, 't is no laughing matter though absurd
If there 's an end of honesty on earth!
La Roque sends letters, lying every word!
Voltaire makes verse, and of himself makes mirth
To the remotest age! Rousseau's the third
Who, driven to despair amid such dearth
Of people that want praising, finds no one
More fit to praise than Paul the simpleton!

CXXIII

"Somebody says—if a man writes at all
It is to show the writer's kith and kin
He was unjustly thought a natural;
And truly, sister, I have yet to win
Your favorable word, it seems, for Paul
Whose poetry you count not worth a pin
Though well enough esteemed by these Voltaires,
Rousseaus and such-like: let them quack, who cares?"

CXXIV

"—To Paris with you, Paul! Not one word's waste

Further: my scrupulosity was vain!
Go triumph! Be my foolish fears effaced
From memory's record! Go, to come again
With glory crowned,—by sister re-embraced,
Cured of that strange delusion of her brain
Which led her to suspect that Paris gloats
On male limbs mostly when in petticoats!"

CXXV

So laughed her last word, with the little touch
Of malice proper to the outraged pride
Of any artist in a work too much
Shorn of its merits. "By all means, be tried
The opposite procedure! Cast your crutch
Away, no longer crippled, nor divide
The credit of your march to the World's Fair
With sister Cherry-cheeks who helped you there!"

CXXVI

Crippled, forsooth! What courser sprightlier pranced
Paris-ward than did Paul? Nay, dreams lent wings:
He flew, or seemed to fly, by dreams entranced.
Dreams? wide-awake realities: no things
Dreamed merely were the missives that advanced
The claim of Malcrais to consort with kings
Crowned by Apollo—not to say with queens
Cinctured by Venus for Idalian scenes.

CXXVII

Soon he arrives, forthwith is found before
The outer gate of glory. Bold tic-toc
Announces there's a giant at the door.
"Ay, sir, here dwells the Chevalier La Roque."
"Lackey! Malcrais—mind, no word less nor more!—
Desires his presence. I've unearthed the brock:
Now, to transfix him!" There stands Paul erect,
Inched out his uttermost, for more effect.

CXXVIII

A bustling entrance: "Idol of my flame!

Can it be that my heart attains at last
Its longing? that you stand, the very same
As in my visions?... Ha! hey, how?" aghast
Stops short the rapture. "Oh, my boy's to blame!
You merely are the messenger! Too fast
My fancy rushed to a conclusion. Pooh!
Well, sir, the lady's substitute is—who?"

CXXIX

Then Paul's smirk grows inordinate. "Shake hands!
Friendship not love awaits you, master mine,
Though nor Malcrais nor any mistress stands
To meet your ardor! So, you don't divine
Who wrote the verses wherewith ring the land's
Whole length and breadth? Just he whereof no line
Had ever leave to blot your Journal—eh?
Paul Desforges Maillard—otherwise Malcrais!"

CXXX

And there the two stood, stare confronting smirk,
A while uncertain which should yield the pas.
In vain the Chevalier beat brain for quirk
To help in this conjuncture; at length, "Bah!
Boh! Since I've made myself a fool, why shirk
The punishment of folly? Ha, ha, ha,
Let me return your handshake!" Comic sock
For tragic buskin prompt thus changed La Roque.

CXXXI

"I'm nobody—a wren-like journalist;
You've flown at higher game and winged your bird,
The golden eagle! That's the grand acquist!
Voltaire's sly Muse, the tiger-cat, has purred.
Prettily round your feet; but if she missed
Priority of stroking, soon were stirred
The dormant spitfire. To Voltaire! away,
Paul Desforges Maillard, otherwise Malcrais!"

CXXXII

Whereupon, arm in arm, and head in air,

The two begin their journey. Need I say,
La Roque had felt the talon of Voltaire,
Had a long-standing little debt to pay,
And pounced, you may depend, on such a rare
Occasion for its due discharge? So, gay
And grenadier-like, marching to assault,
They reach the enemy's abode, there halt.

CXXXIII

"I'll be announcer!" quoth La Roque: "I know,
Better than you, perhaps, my Breton bard,
How to procure an audience! He's not slow
To smell a rat, this scamp Voltaire! Discard
The petticoats too soon,—you'll never show
Your haut-de-chausses and all they've made or marred
In your true person. Here's his servant. Pray,
Will the great man see Demoiselle Malcrais?"

CXXXIV

Now, the great man was also, no whit less,
The man of self-respect,—more great man he!
And bowed to social usage, dressed the dress,
And decorated to the fit degree
His person; 't was enough to bear the stress
Of battle in the field, without, when free
From outside foes, inviting friends' attack
By—sword in hand? No,—ill-made coat on back.

CXXXV

And, since the announcement of his visitor
Surprised him at his toilet,—never glass
Had such solicitation! "Black, now—or
Brown be the killing wig to wear? Alas,
Where's the rouge gone, this cheek were better for
A tender touch of? Melted to a mass,
All my pomatum! There 's at all events
A devil—for he's got among my scents!"

CXXXVI

So, "barbered ten times o'er," as Antony

Paced to his Cleopatra, did at last
Voltaire proceed to the fair presence: high
In color, proud in port, as if a blast
Of trumpet bade the world "Take note! draws nigh
To Beauty, Power! Behold the Iconoclast,
The Poet, the Philosopher, the Rod
Of iron for imposture! Ah my God!"

CXXXVII

For there stands smirking Paul, and—what lights fierce
The situation as with sulphur flash—
There grinning stands La Roque! No carte-and-tierce
Observes the grinning fencer, but, full dash
From breast to shoulder-blade, the thrusts transpierce
That armor against which so idly clash
The swords of priests and pedants! Victors there,
Two smirk and grin who have befooled—Voltaire!

CXXXVIII

A moment's horror; then quick turn-about
On high-heeled shoe,—flurry of ruffles, flounce
Of wig-ties and of coat-tails,—and so out
Of door banged wrathfully behind, goes—bounce—
Voltaire in tragic exit! vows, no doubt,
Vengeance upon the couple. Did he trounce
Either, in point of fact? His anger's flash
subsided if a culprit craved his cash.

CXXXIX

As for La Roque, he having laughed his laugh
To heart's content,—the joke defunct at once,
Dead in the birth, you see,—its epitaph
Was sober earnest. "Well, sir, for the nonce,
You 've gained the laurel; never hope to graff
A second sprig of triumph there! Ensconce
Yourself again at Croisic: let it be
Enough you mastered both Voltaire and—me!

CXL

"Don't linger here in Paris to parade

Your victory, and have the very boys
Point at you! 'There 's the little mouse which made
Believe those two big lions that its noise,
Nibbling away behind the hedge, conveyed
Intelligence that—portent which destroys
All courage in the lion's heart, with horn
That's fable—there lay couched the unicorn!'

CXLI

"Beware us, now we 've found who fooled us! Quick
To cover! 'In proportion to men's fright,
Expect their fright's revenge!' quoth politic
Old Macchiavelli. As for me,—all's right:
I'm but a journalist. But no pin's prick
The tooth leaves when Voltaire is roused to bite!
So, keep your counsel, I advise! Adieu!
Good journey I Ha, ha, ha, Malcrais was—you!"

CXLII

"—Yes, I 'm Malcrais, and somebody beside,
You snickering monkey!" thus winds up the tale
Our hero, safe at home, to that black-eyed
Cherry-cheeked sister, as she soothes the pale
Mortified poet. "Let their worst be tried,
I'm their match henceforth—very man and male!
Don't talk to me of knocking-under! man
And male must end what petticoats began!

CXLIII

"How woman-like it is to apprehend
The world will eat its words! why, words transfixed
To stone, they stare at you in print,—at end,
Each writer's style and title! Choose betwixt
Fool and knave for his name, who should intend
To perpetrate a baseness so unmixed
With prospect of advantage! What is writ
Is writ: they've praised me, there's an end of it!

CXLIV

"No, Dear, allow me! I shall print these same

Pieces, with no omitted line, as Paul's.
Malcrais no longer, let me see folk blame
What they—praised simply?—placed on pedestals,
Each piece a statue in the House of Fame!
Fast will they stand there, though their presence galls
The envious crew: such show their teeth, perhaps,
And snarl, but never bite! I know the chaps!"

CXLV

O Paul, oh, piteously deluded! Pace
Thy sad sterility of Croisic flats,
Watch, from their southern edge, the foamy race
Of high-tide as it heaves the drowning mats
Of yellow-berried web-growth from their place,
The rock-ridge, when, rolling as far as Batz,
One broadside crashes on it, and the crags,
That needle under, stream with weedy rags!

CXLVI

Or, if thou wilt, at inland Bergerac,
Rude heritage but recognized domain,
Do as two here are doing: make hearth crack
With logs until thy chimney roar again
Jolly with fire-glow! Let its angle lack
No grace of Cherry-cheeks thy sister, fain
To do a sister's office and laugh smooth
Thy corrugated brow—that scowls forsooth!

CXLVII

Wherefore? Who does not know how these La Roques,
Voltaires, can say and unsay, praise and blame,
Prove black white, white black, play at paradox
And, when they seem to lose it, win the game?
Care not thou what this badger, and that fox,
His fellow in rascality, call "fame!"
Fiddlepin's end! Thou hadst it,—quack, quack, quack!
Have quietude from geese at Bergerac!

CXLVIII

Quietude! For, be very sure of this!
A twelvemonth hence, and men shall know or care

As much for what to-day they clap or hiss
As for the fashion of the wigs they wear,
Then wonder at. There's fame which, bale or bliss,—
Got by no gracious word of great Voltaire
Or not-so-great La Roque,—is taken back
By neither, any more than Bergerac!

CXLIX

Too true! or rather, true as ought to be!
No more of Paul the man, Malcrais the maid,
Thenceforth forever! One or two, I see,
Stuck by their poet: who the longest stayed
Was Jean-Baptiste Rousseau, and even he
Seemingly saddened as perforce he paid
A rhyming tribute: "After death, survive—
He hoped he should: and died while yet alive!"

CL

No, he hoped nothing of the kind, or held
His peace and died in silent good old age.
Him it was, curiosity impelled
To seek if there were extant still some page
Of his great predecessor, rat who belled
The cat once, and would never deign engage
In after-combat with mere mice,—saved from
More sonneteering.—René Gentilhomme.

CLI

Paul's story furnished forth that famous play
Of Piron's "Métromanie:" there you 'll find
He 's Francaleu, while Demoiselle Malcrais
Is Demoiselle No-end-of-names-behind!
As for Voltaire, he's Damis. Good and gay
The plot and dialogue, and all 's designed
To spite Voltaire: at "Something" such the laugh
Of simply "Nothing!" (see his epitaph).

CLII

But truth, truth, that's the gold! and all the good
I find in fancy is, it serves to set

Gold's inmost glint free, gold which comes up rude
And rayless from the mine. All fume and fret
Of artistry beyond this point pursued
Brings out another sort of burnish: yet
Always the ingot has its very own
Value, a sparkle struck from truth alone.

CLIII

Now, take this sparkle and the other spirt
Of fitful flame,—twin births of our gray brand
That 's sinking fast to ashes! I assert,
As sparkles want but fuel to expand
Into a conflagration no mere squirt
Will quench too quickly, so might Croisic strand,
Had Fortune pleased posterity to chowse,
Boast of her brace or beacons luminous.

CLIV

Did earlier Agamemnons lack their bard?
But later bards lacked Agamemnon too!
How often frustrate they of fame's award
Just because Fortune, as she listed, blew
Some slight bark's sails to bellying, mauled and marred
And forced to put about the First-rate True,
Such tacks but for a time: still—small-craft ride
At anchor, rot while Beddoes breasts the tide!

CLV

Dear, shall I tell you? There 's a simple test
Would serve, when people take on them to weigh
The worth of poets. "Who was better, best,
This, that, the other bard?" (Bards none gainsay
As good, observe! no matter for the rest.)
"What quality preponderating may
Turn the scale as it trembles?" End the strife
By asking "Which one led a happy life?"

CLVI

If one did, over his antagonist
That yelled or shrieked or sobbed or wept or wailed

Or simply had the dumps,—dispute who list,—
I count him victor. Where his fellow failed,
Mastered by his own means of might,—acquist
Of necessary sorrows,—he prevailed,
A strong since joyful man who stood distinct
Above slave-sorrows to his chariot linked.

CLVII

Was not his lot to feel more? What meant "feel"
Unless to suffer! Not, to see more? Sight—
What helped it but to watch the drunken reel
Of vice and folly round him, left and right,
One dance of rogues and idiots! Not, to deal
More with things lovely? What provoked the spite
Of filth incarnate, like the poet's need
Of other nutriment than strife and greed!

CLVIII

Who knows most, doubts most; entertaining hope,
Means recognizing fear; the keener sense
Of all comprised within our actual scope
Recoils from aught beyond earth's dim and dense.
Who, grown familiar with the sky, will grope
Henceforward among groundlings? That's offence
Just as indubitably: stars abound
O'erhead, but then—what flowers make glad the ground!

CLIX

So, force is sorrow, and each sorrow, force:
What then? since Swiftness gives the charioteer
The palm, his hope be in the vivid horse
Whose neck God clothed with thunder, not the steer
Sluggish and safe! Yoke Hatred, Crime, Remorse,
Despair: but ever 'mid the whirling fear,
Let, through the tumult, break the poet's face
Radiant, assured his wild slaves win the race!

CLX

Therefore I say ... no, shall not say, but think,
And save my breath for better purpose. White

From gray our log has burned to: just one blink
That quivers, loth to leave it, as a sprite
The outworn body. Ere your eyelids' wink
Punish who sealed so deep into the night
Your mouth up, for two poets dead so long,—
Here pleads a live pretender: right your wrong!

What a pretty tale you told me
Once upon a time
—Said you found it somewhere (scold me!)
Was it prose or was it rhyme,
Greek or Latin? Greek, you said,
While your shoulder propped my head.

Anyhow there 's no forgetting
This much if no more,
That a poet (pray, no petting!)
Yes, a bard, sir, famed of yore,
Went where suchlike used to go,
Singing for a prize, you know.

Well, he had to sing, nor merely
Sing but play the lyre;
Playing was important clearly
Quite as singing: I desire,
Sir, you keep the fact in mind
For a purpose that 's behind.

There stood he, while deep attention
Held the judges round,
—Judges able, I should mention,
To detect the slightest sound
Sung or played amiss: such ears
Had old judges, it appears!

None the less he sang out boldly,
Played in time and tune,
Till the judges, weighing coldly
Each note's worth, seemed, late or soon,
Sure to smile "In vain one tries
Picking faults out: take the prize!"

When, a mischief! Were they seven
Strings the lyre possessed?
Oh, and afterwards eleven,
Thank you! Well, sir,—who had guessed
Such ill luck in store?—it happed

One of those same seven strings snapped.

All was lost, then! No! a cricket
(What "cicada"? Pooh!)
—Some mad thing that left its thicket
For mere love of music—flew
With its little heart on fire,
Lighted on the crippled lyre.

So that when (Ah, joy!) our singer
For his truant string
Feels with disconcerted finger,
What does cricket else but fling
Fiery heart forth, sound the note
Wanted by the throbbing throat?

Ay and, ever to the ending,
Cricket chirps at need,
Executes the hand's intending,
Promptly, perfectly,—indeed
Saves the singer from defeat
With her chirrup low and sweet.

Till, at ending, all the judges
Cry with one assent
"Take the prize—a prize who grudges
Such a voice and instrument?
Why, we took your lyre for harp,
So it shrilled us forth F sharp!"

Did the conqueror spurn the creature,
Once its service done?
That's no such uncommon feature
In the case when Music's son
Finds his Lotte's power too spent
For aiding soul-development.

No! This other, on returning
Homeward, prize in hand,
Satisfied his bosom's yearning:
(Sir, I hope you understand!)
—Said "Some record there must be
Of this cricket's help to me!"

So, he made himself a statue:
Marble stood, life-size;
On the lyre, he pointed at you,
Perched his partner in the prize;

Never more apart you found
Her, he throned, from him, she crowned.

That 's the tale: its application?
Somebody I know
Hopes one day for reputation
Through his poetry that 's—Oh,
All so learned and so wise
And deserving of a prize!

If he gains one, will some ticket,
When his statue 's built,
Tell the gazer "'T was a cricket
Helped my crippled lyre, whose lilt
Sweet and low, when strength usurped
Softness' place i' the scale, she chirped?

"For as victory was nighest,
While I sang and played,—
With my lyre at lowest, highest,
Right alike,—one string that made
'Love' sound soft was snapt in twain,
Never to be heard again,—

"Had not a kind cricket fluttered,
Perched upon the place
Vacant left, and duly uttered
'Love, Love, Love,' whene'er the bass
Asked the treble to atone
For its somewhat sombre drone."

But you don't know music! Wherefore
Keep on casting pearls
To a—poet? All I care for
Is—to tell him that a girl's
"Love" comes aptly in when gruff
Grows his singing. (There, enough!)

OH LOVE! LOVE

Translation of a lyric in the Hyppolytus of Euripides, and printed by J. P. Mahaffy in his Euripides, 1879.
Mr. Mahaffy writes: "Mr. Browning has honored me with the following translation of these stanzas, so
that the general reader may not miss the meaning or the spirit of the ode. The English metre, though not
a strict reproduction, gives an excellent idea of the original."

I

Oh Love! Love, thou that from the eyes diffusest
Yearning, and on the soul sweet grace inducest—
Souls against whom thy hostile march is made—
Never to me be manifest in ire,
Nor, out of time and tune, my peace invade!
Since neither from the fire—
No, nor from the stars—is launched a bolt more mighty
Than that of Aphrodité
Hurled from the hands of Love, the boy with Zeus for sire.

II

Idly, how idly, by the Alpheian river
And in the Pythian shrines of Phœbus, quiver
Blood-offerings from the bull, which Hellas heaps:
While Love we worship not—the Lord of men!
Worship not him, the very key who keeps
Of Aphrodité, when
She closes up her dearest chamber-portals:
—Love, when he comes to mortals,
Wide-wasting, through those deeps of woes beyond the deep!

Robert Browning – A Short Biography

He is the equal of any Victorian Poet that could be mentioned. However, Browning continues to be in the shadow of Tennyson, Arnold, Hopkins, Morris and many others.

Robert Browning was born on May 7th, 1812 in Walworth in the parish of Camberwell, London. He was baptized on June 14th, 1812, at Lock's Fields Independent Chapel, York Street, Walworth.

Browning's early years were certainly very interesting. His mother was an excellent pianist and a very devout evangelical Christian. His father, who worked as a clerk at the Bank of England, was also an artist, scholar, antiquarian, and collector of books and pictures. Indeed, he amassed more than 6,000 volumes of rare books including works in Greek, Hebrew, Latin, French, Italian, and Spanish. For the young and curious Browning, it was a wonderful resource, added to which his father was a guiding force in his education.

Many accounts attest that Browning was already proficient at reading and writing by the age of five. He is said to have been a bright but anxious student and to have studied and learnt Latin, Greek, and French by the time he was fourteen. From fourteen to sixteen he was educated at home, tutored in music, drawing, dancing, and horsemanship. Certainly, language and the arts were two areas the young Browning both absorbed and pushed himself towards.

At the age of twelve he wrote a volume of Byronic verse he called Incondita, which his parents attempted to have published. The attempts were unsuccessful and, disappointed, Browning destroyed the work.

In 1825, a cousin gave Browning a collection of Percy Bysshe Shelley's poetry; Browning was so enamored with the poems that he asked for the rest of Shelley's works for his thirteenth birthday. In fact, Browning then went the extra mile, declaring himself to be both a vegetarian and an atheist in honour of his hero.

Intriguingly it seems that the rejection of his first volume didn't dim his appreciation of other poets, but it appears to have stopped him writing any poems between the ages of thirteen and twenty.

In 1828, Browning enrolled at the newly-opened University of London. He was uncomfortable with the experience and he soon left, anxious to read and absorb at his own pace.

His education which, overall is notably rambling and lacks a structure that many of his artistic contemporaries enjoyed, i.e. excellent public schooling and then a degree at Oxford or Cambridge, may present many of his critics with ammunition to criticize, but alternatively his hap-hazard education certainly contributed to many of the references that baffled both critics and his audience, but they tellingly show the breath and scale of what he could turn words too. What others would call obscure references were, to Browning, remarkably obvious.

Browning's early career was very promising. His long poem Pauline (of which only a fragment was ever finished and published) brought him to the attention of the Pre-Raphaelite master Dante Gabriel Rossetti and his difficult Paracelsus (published in 1835) was warmly admired by both Dickens and Wordsworth.

In the 1830s he met the actor William Macready and was encouraged to develop and turn his talents to the stage by writing verse drama. But these plays, including Strafford, which ran for five nights in 1837, and those contained within the Bells and Pomegranates series, were, for the most part, unsuccessful.

During this period Browning began to discover that his real talents lay in taking a single character and allowing that character to discover more about himself by revealing further personal aspects of himself in his speeches; the dramatic monologue. The techniques he developed through this—especially the use of diction, rhythm, and symbol—are regarded as his most important contribution to poetry. They would later influence such major poets of the 20th Century as Ezra Pound, T. S. Eliot, and Robert Frost.

By 1840, with the publication of Sordello, the tide turned somewhat. Many thought he was being deliberately obscure, opaque beyond measure and his poetry for the next decade or so was not eagerly acquired or talked about.

As Browning attempted to rehabilitate his career he began a relationship with Elizabeth Barrett in 1845. He had read her poems and, being totally charmed by their quality, was determined to meet her. The poetess was better known than the younger Browning but suffered from a debilitating illness and was also subject to the harsh behaviour of her over-bearing father. Nevertheless, the new couple were soon inseparable.

Her father, as he did with any of his children that married, disinherited her. Despite this she had some money from her own resources and sensing that the best outcome for both the relationship and her own health was to move abroad the couple did just that. After a private marriage at St Marylebone Parish Church, in September 1846, they journeyed to Europe to honeymoon in Paris.

Their new life now took them to Italy, first to Pisa and a little later to Florence. There they absorbed life and one another.

But in the short term the literary assault on Browning's work did not let up. He was now criticized by such patrician writers as Charles Kingsley for his abandonment of England for foreign lands. Browning could do little to answer these attacks except to compose with his pen and continue with his poetical journey.

The Browning's were well respected, and even famous. Elizabeth health began to improve, she grew stronger and in 1849, at the age of 43, between four miscarriages, she gave birth to a son, Robert Wiedeman Barrett Browning, whom they nicknamed "Penini" or "Pen",

Intriguingly despite his growing reputation and return to form as a poet he was more often than not known as 'Elizabeth Barrett's husband'.

Work flowed from his pen that was to ensure his reputation as one of England's leading poets. When his collection Men and Women was published in 1855 it contained some of his finest lines. It was dedicated to Elizabeth. Life had begun to smile handsome rewards upon the Brownings.

Victorian society was very much taken with all things spiritualist. It was not enough to have command of much of the globe through Empire, they wished to know and explore wherever they could. The spirit world beckoned their interest. Browning dissented from this view believing it was all a hoax and a fraud. Elizabeth, however, was inclined to believe and this caused several disagreements between the couple.

They attended a séance by Daniel Dunglas Home, in July 1855. (Home was a famous and clamored after Scottish physical medium with the reported ability to levitate and speak with the dead). It is said that during this séance a spirit face materialised. Home then claimed it was the face of Browning's son who had died in infancy. Browning seized the 'materialisation' which turned out to be Home's bare foot. Browning had never lost a son in infancy.

After the séance, Browning wrote an angry letter to The Times, in which he said: "the whole display of hands, spirit utterances etc., was a cheat and imposture."

The Browning's time in Italy were immensely rewarding years for both their personal and professional lives. Browning encouraged her to include Sonnets from the Portuguese in her published works, these beautiful poems are undoubtedly one of the highlights of English love poetry.

Elizabeth had become quite politicised during these years. Engrossed in Italian politics (which was continuing to slowly re-unify the country), she issued a small volume of political poems entitled Poems before Congress (1860) most of which were written to express her sympathy with the Italian cause after the earlier outbreak of The Second Italian Independence War in 1859. In England they caused uproar. Conservative magazines such as Blackwood's and the Saturday Review labelled her a fanatic. She dedicated the book to her husband.

But in 1861 tragedy struck.

The couple had spent the winter of 1860–61 in Rome when Elizabeth's health deteriorated again and they returned to Florence in early June. However, these turned out to be her final weeks. Only morphine would now still the pain. She died in Browning's arms on June 29th, 1861. Browning said that she died "smilingly, happily, and with a face like a girl's .... Her last word was .... "Beautiful".

Her burial took place in the nearby Protestant English Cemetery of Florence. The local people were deeply saddened, and shops closed their doors in grief and respect.

Browning and their son were obviously devastated. Unable to bear being in Florence without Elizabeth they soon returned to London to live at 19 Warwick Crescent, Maida Vale.

As he re-integrated himself back into the London literary scene he began to finally receive the proper praise, respect and reputation that his works deserved.

Browning went on to publish Dramatis Personæ (1864), and The Ring and the Book (1868–1869). The latter, based on an "old yellow book" which told of a seventeenth-century Italian murder trial, received wide and generous critical acclaim. Although by now he was in the twilight of a long and prolific career, that had achieved some notable ups and downs, he was respected and indeed renowned for his talents and works.

In 1878, he revisited Italy for the first time since Elizabeth's death. He would return there on several further occasions but never to Florence.

Such was the esteem he was held in that The Browning Society was founded in 1881. Although he had never obtained a degree (something that set him apart from many other Victorian poets) he was now awarded honorary degrees from Oxford University in 1882 and then the University of Edinburgh in 1884.

In 1887, Browning produced the major work of his later years, Parleyings with Certain People of Importance in Their Day. Browning now spoke with his own voice as he engaged in a series of dialogues with long-forgotten figures of literary, artistic, and philosophic history. Unfortunately, both the critics and public were completely baffled by this.

On April 7th, 1889 Browning attended a dinner party at the home of his friend, the artist Rudolf Lehmann. The highlight of which was a recording made on a wax cylinder on an Edison cylinder phonograph. On the recording, which still exists, Browning recites part of How They Brought the Good News from Ghent to Aix, and can even be heard apologising when he forgets the words.

The recording was first played in 1890 on the anniversary of his death, at a gathering of his admirers, it was said to be the first time anyone's voice 'had been heard from beyond the grave'.

His last work Asolando: Fancies and Facts (1889), returned to his brief and concise lyric verse that was so popular. It was published on the day of his death on December 12th, 1889, Robert Browning was at his son's home Ca' Rezzonico in Venice.

He was buried in Poets' Corner in Westminster Abbey; his grave lies immediately adjacent to that of Alfred Tennyson.

Among the many who have publicly acknowledged their literary debt to him are Henry James, Oscar Wilde, George Bernard Shaw, G. K. Chesterton, Ezra Pound, Jorge Luis Borges, and Vladimir Nabokov.

Robert Browning - A Concise Bibliography

Here follows a list of the plays and poetry volumes published during his lifetime. Poems of particular worth are noted from within those volumes.

Pauline: A Fragment of a Confession (1833)
Paracelsus (1835)
Strafford (play) (1837)
Sordello (1840)
Bells and Pomegranates No. I: Pippa Passes (play) (1841)
      The Year's at the Spring
Bells and Pomegranates No. II: King Victor and King Charles (play) (1842)
Bells and Pomegranates No. III: Dramatic Lyrics (1842)
      Porphyria's Lover
      Soliloquy of the Spanish Cloister
      My Last Duchess
      The Pied Piper of Hamelin
      Count Gismond
      Johannes Agricola in Meditation
Bells and Pomegranates No. IV: The Return of the Druses (play) (1843)
Bells and Pomegranates No. V: A Blot in the 'Scutcheon (play) (1843)
Bells and Pomegranates No. VI: Colombe's Birthday (play) (1844)
Bells and Pomegranates No. VII: Dramatic Romances and Lyrics (1845)
      The Laboratory
      How They Brought the Good News from Ghent to Aix
      The Bishop Orders His Tomb at Saint Praxed's Church
      The Lost Leader
      Home Thoughts from Abroad
      Meeting at Night
Bells and Pomegranates No. VIII: Luria and A Soul's Tragedy (plays) (1846)
Christmas-Eve and Easter-Day (1850)
An Essay on Percy Bysshe Shelley (essay) (1852)
Two Poems (1854)
Men and Women (1855)
      Love Among the Ruins
      A Toccata of Galuppi's
      Childe Roland to the Dark Tower Came
      Fra Lippo Lippi
      Andrea Del Sarto
      The Patriot

www.ingramcontent.com/pod-product-compliance
Lightning Source LLC
Chambersburg PA
CBHW060051050426
42448CB00011B/2404